◆ HOW TO ROCK CLIMB ◆

Face
Climbing

◆ HOW TO ROCK CLIMB ◆

Face
Climbing

John Long

CHOCKSTONE PRESS

Evergreen, Colorado
1991

HOW TO ROCK CLIMB: FACE CLIMBING

COVER PHOTOS:

(front) Louisa Jovane on "Churning in the Wake," Smith Rock; photo by Greg Epperson

(back, top) Lynn Hill at a World Cup competition at Nimes, France; photo by Beth Wald.

(back, bottom) Climbers on the Ten Pins, Needles of South Dakota; photo by Beth Wald.

All uncredited photos were taken by Kevin Powell.

ISBN 0-934641-36-6

PUBLISHED AND DISTRIBUTED BY
Chockstone Press, Inc.
Post Office Box 3505
Evergreen, Colorado 80439

Other books by John Long:
Gorilla Monsoon
How to Rock Climb
How to Rock Climb: Climbing Anchors

Acknowledgements

Credit to all those who wrote something for this manual: Bob Gaines, Rick Accomazzo, Kevin Powell, Darrell Hensel, Mari Gingery, Christian Griffith, Russ Walling, John Sherman, Scott Cosgrove, Hans Florine, Troy Mayr, Alison Osius, John Bachar, Nancy Pritchard, Lynn Hill and Eric Horst. Most agree that they learned something by putting into words what had long been instinctual. I trust we'll all be better climbers for their efforts. Likewise, thanks to photographer/climber Kevin Powell, who spend many weekends doing the near-impossible job of capturing on film what face climbing is all about. And a million dollars and a condo in Crete for Chockstone Press editor Tracy Salcedo, who caught and corrected my few thousand mistakes and oversights.

Publisher George Meyers first suggested this manual, and I regret to say that we never once came to blows about anything. I hammered out my part, and George did the other 90 percent – the layout, photo culling, general organizing and grief-bearing.

Warning

This is an instruction book to a potentially dangerous activity. It is not intended to be the only source of information for those wishing to pursue the sport of rock climbing. This book assumes prior and competent knowledge in the use of various climbing safety devices. Supplemental instruction by certified rock climbing instructors is necessary to obtain the safest use of this book. By the use of this book, the reader hereby releases the author, publisher, and distributor from liability for any injury, including death, that might result.

Bob Gaines photo

C O N T E N T S

FACE CLIMBING

JOHN LONG

The Art of Face Climbing

New energy, refined technique, superior equipment, fresh notions of what is possible – each new generation brings these to the climbing game, primary elements that enable them to improve, at least technically, on the past. Active climbers always have sought out the new and the harder. And whatever our own level, we routinely try to outdo our last performance. Striving toward that higher, steeper peak has remained central to the game since Whymper climbed the Matterhorn. Such is the spirit in all sports.

But climbing is more than mere sport, and the present-day climber's alliance with the past might stop with his desire to always do something harder. He probably has a totally different orientation than climbers of the 70s, or even the 80s. However independent, climbers still form a loose group who share a heritage, a literature and role models at the top. And those at the top have changed dramatically in the past 20 years, particularly in terms of why they are climbing, their motivation to continue and their methods of ascent. As with all sports, attitudes from the top forever trickle down into the mainstream, affecting the current of the whole game.

The 60s climber was equal parts renegade, daredevil, bohemian and athlete. A climber from that 'Golden Era' most likely was drawn to climbing through backpacking, scrambling, skiing, or simply a love for the outdoors. To a great extent, his climbing was cherished as much for its interface with nature as for the trials and stimulation of moving on the rock. Climbing simply put some radical voltage into his wilderness experience. But that generation changed things quickly and forever.

The 60s were loaded with highly skilled and motivated climbers, and the standards they established required of the next generation – if it was to up the technical ante – something more than just a simple love of sky and trees. Robbins, Pratt, Frost, Kor, Chouinard, Kamps, Sacherer – these guys were real, and their climbs are formidable to this day. So the climber of the 70s had to reorient himself if he was to push things further along. To that end, the following generation approached climbing as a serious athletic endeavor. That is not to say that the 70s climber was something more than a flat-broke nonconformist, it's just that he probably came to climbing through baseball, wrestling, or some other sport.

By 1975, the hardest climbs were so severe that someone lacking natural athletic skills, not actively climbing with

(opposite)
Troy Mayr on "I Have the Touch," 5.12c/d, Joshua Tree.

Ron Wolfe photo

intensity and not focused heart and soul on climbing rock had little or no chance of scaling the true test pieces. It was during the 70s that leading climbers first went after impossibly hard free climbs, and these climbs – the successful ones – were little less than significant athletic undertakings in the context of all sports.

Once top climbers started thinking of climbing in terms of world-class athletics, it was certain that the milieu of 'proper' sports would enter into the game – namely, outright competition. Around 1980, Europeans – particularly the French – began staging climbing competitions. It took some years to work out the format, which eventually eschewed climbing on actual rock, focusing instead on man-made climbs scaled during indoor competitions. For better or worse, these competitions had about as much to do with the great outdoors as a canasta tournament. Cracks were virtually impossible to replicate artificially, so the climbs were, and continue to be, mostly nasty face routes ascending man-made walls, following strings of glued or bolted-on artificial face holds.

"Freakin' Fred" glides up "Old 5.10," a 70s face route in Yosemite

Concurrently, in the out of doors, top climbers increasingly were moving away from difficult cracks and onto the open face. At the more popular climbing areas, most crack lines, however obscure, had already been climbed. Furthermore, if the climbers of the 70s did not establish the technical crack limit, they certainly approached it. For these two reasons – the scarcity of new cracks to climb and the fact that the outer envelope of crack climbing had already been broached – climbers started tackling bald faces that previous generations had entirely overlooked, or had written off as too contrived. In short, the new generation wanted to do harder climbs, and they found the challenge on these hold-bereft faces. World-class climbers no longer went exclusively to Yosemite, the crack capitol of the world, but started frequenting those areas where remarkably hard face climbs were the norm. By the early 80s, the world's hardest climbs were face routes. For most climbers, the days of knickers and salami were long gone. It was all Spandex jumpsuits and amino supplements. In some cases, the only thing a present-day climber shares with the past is his upward movement and the desire to do harder and harder projects.

Whenever something changes radically, there always is a trade off – something gained, something lost. Today's hardest face climbs are technically harder than those of the past. No one questions that. But this technical superiority comes at the expense of outright adventure and jeopardy, two elements of the past which, even as late as 1980, were

Stefan Glowacz on "To Bolt or Not to Be," a 5.14a at Smith Rock

Beth Wald photo

regarded as positively essential to 'real' climbing. But however real, once the ground-up ethic started impeding the quest for greater difficulty, the old norms were for the most part abandoned by those on the leading edge. Simply, the old ethics were holding people back. Hitherto, hang-dogging, toproping, pre-placing protection, etc., were not unheard of techniques, but were certainly not accepted by the mainstream. The end always was qualified by the means, and if traditional values were ignored, many considered the route invalid. In truth, when the hardest routes were still flashable, we had the luxury of 'pure' ethics. Once the routes started requiring days, even weeks, to work out, the old ethics were judged impractical, and slowly abandoned.

Hangdogging: resting on the rope to study the moves

The first move was to factor out jeopardy by arranging ready protection, oftentimes installed via a toprope. The emphasis was now on explosive, gymnastic moves that were hard enough without the added onus of physical harm. So if anything can be said about the modern, rather generic term 'sportclimbing,' it's that the game is a comparatively safe one, focused on difficulty for difficulty's sake. With some of these new test pieces – where every toe hold is chalked, every move memorized – the climb has been reduced to a phenomenal physical challenge, but little more. Certainly, these new bohemians don't brave the same risks climbers used to face every time they went to the crags. Add to this the fact that for some, the ultimate expression is ascending a 50-foot fiberglass wall in an indoor arena before 1,000 rabid fans, and it's no wonder some top climbers feel they are climbing inside a bottle. (There are still some bold routes going up, but they are the exception, and tend to be far easier than those at the technical limit.)

This new craze has its merits – novelty, the fervor of head-to-head competition, and the exhibition of consummate athletic skill – but look for climbers to start applying their technical advances to projects beyond fiberglass walls and short, sieged routes. Don't forget, there'll be another generation coming along soon, looking to up the ante. It's only logical that they'll take techniques honed on artificial walls and short routes and apply them to big, bold climbs. Bank on it. There's nowhere else to go.

But, for now, a keen climber might be motivated by the grim routes on the competitive circuit. Likewise, he might aspire to the 5.14 routes at the New River Gorge, or any number of other areas renowned for bleak face climbing. In a word, face climbing has taken over the sport in terms of popularity and prestige. Even weekend warriors are moving onto the face in greater numbers, and gear manufacturers are taking note. Most every new wrinkle in each year's batch of rock shoes has extreme face climbing in mind. Face climbing simply is the technique of choice these days, particularly bolt-protected routes that require only a small rack of quickdraws – 'clip-and-go' routes. This is not the case across the board, but protection on the very hardest climbs has virtually eliminated the need for the art of protecting the leader; and even the concepts of boldness and risk have, for the most part, been cast aside in pursuit of the human limit.

The increased popularity of face climbing and ever-rising standards have resulted in countless revisions in style and technique. Starting at the rudimentary level, *Face Climbing* will embrace the art of face climbing and track it up to the hardest face routes currently climbed. Insofar as some of America's outstanding climbers have contributed to the text, this book should address the needs of both the novice interested in a fundamental understanding of technique, and the hotshot who is always looking to pick up another trick. This book is *not* a beginner's guide to rock climbing. It assumes a sound understanding of the tenets of rope management and climbing technique.

ATTITUDE

There was some small objection that in my instructional book, *How to Rock Climb!*, I encouraged beginners to aspire after great things. The arguments claimed that novice climbers actually are discouraged and intimated by pictures, narratives and general mention of world-class climbs; that they were made to feel inferior if they didn't strive after the hard stuff, and that encouragement to this end is really so much elitism. I assumed, and still believe, that all climbers need dreams, and that whether one man's dream is to climb, say, the South Face of Washington Column (which has been scaled no less than 2,000 times, by blind climbers, amputees, et. al.), or to establish new wall climbs in the Karokoram, or to win the European competitive circuit, it is only fruitful and human to strive to be your best. Furthermore, I tried to instill the idea that how far a climber goes is absolutely up to him. Most anyone can climb the South Face of the Column, if they go after it in a measured way. There is no mystery. No nostrums are required. Desire and dedication are the keys; your only limitation is the size of your dreams. Throughout videos and different instruction manuals, I have always skewed things toward the aspiring climber, because we're all aspiring climbers to some degree.

One of our most stubborn myths is that by encouraging a climber to go for the gold, said climber unwittingly will get in over his head and suffer an injury as a consequence. This is rubbish for two reasons. Technical difficulty does not translate to more dangerous climbing, especially on today's new-age face routes, which often are bolted from bottom to top. A climber gets hurt because he overlooked basic safety procedures, or perhaps because of plain bad luck – neither of which has a thing to do with technical difficulties. Accident reports bear me out here. How many of these accounts conclude that a climber tried a route technically too difficult for him and got hurt as a consequence? None. And secondly, what's wrong with trying something that supposedly is too hard for you? It can be instructive. Not to mention that half the time the climber succeeds. Observe the safety procedures and go for it. So what if you fall off? Join the club, buddy. Ask any accomplished climber how many leader falls he's taken and he'll need a calculator to figure it out. I'm not suggesting a climber be reckless or unrealistic. A 5.8 climber would be ill-advised to try to lead a poorly-protected 5.11 route. It's all a matter of common sense and small increments. For example, a 5.8 leader should never shy away from a 5.9 climb simply because of the higher number.

If you're not interested in pushing yourself, if you never want to fall, if you're out to cruise moderate routes and simply enjoy yourself, by God do so. If someone badgers you to step things up and you don't feel like it, tell the cad to wash your car, or mow your lawn. What a climber does – within reason – is absolutely his own affair, and you should respect this. Some climbers get too hung up on high numbers, as though cranking a hard route affirms they are superior beings deserving preferential treatment. Hogwash. Let's not loose sight of the fact that we're talking about climbing rocks, not harnessing fusion or saving the rain forest. Nonetheless, the idea we shouldn't encourage the willing, in deference to the unwilling, is something I'll dismiss straightaway.

A book can only be judged according to its aims. So let's state clearly that this book is geared specifically towards the climber – novice or expert – who wants to improve. Some may desire to climb world-class routes; others simply may want to enjoy more control at whatever level he chooses to climb. Hopefully, both can learn something by reading this text.

IT'S JUST A BOOK

I am neither the greatest climber or the greatest writer in the world. Not even my mother thinks so. But even if I was, you could never learn how to face climb solely by reading this manual.

With the help of a handful of America's outstanding face climbers, I have tried to provide you with a little bag of tangible tricks that can improve your climbing. To discuss the general theories on face climbing – well, the topic is so nebulous that I might as well be talking about how to play the guitar. You can teach someone the manifold picking techniques and how to play all the chords, but this is no guarantee the student will go on to play music. Hence, this book can only hope to be a guide to proper form.

You learn how to face climb by face climbing. Each climber is, essentially, self-taught. As you climb more, you intuitively learn how to best perform. Though you may not consciously realize every little subtlety of your moves, your body knows well what works best. So the real value of this manual is just this: By studying all the material discussed herein, you most likely will be gaining a new, or clearer, understanding of techniques which, to some extent, you already know and already are using in your climbing. The point is to become consciously aware of all the various skills; to understand all the basic principles in plain English; to verify, if you will, what your body already knows, or eventually will learn. By indelibly stamping the precepts of good technique into your memory, your conscious awareness of them is increased as is your likelihood of using them. So, in this sense, this book can serve, at the least, as a sound reminder.

(opposite)
Terri Peterson dances up
"Loose Lady" (5.10b),
Joshua Tree

Greg Epperson photo

Every type of face climbing can be approached from several perspectives: The purely technical aspect, which concerns only the actual climbing and physical movement; the strategy aspect, which concerns all the tactics, both physical and mental; and the tricks of the trade, dealing with special insights, etc. I also could throw in a fourth bit on ropework and protection, but this is not the domain of this book, which is principally a treatise on physical movement and mental preparedness. Granted, protecting the leader is a complicated and essential affair. Unfortunately, however, aside from the protection fundamentals laid down in *How to Rock Climb!*, there is little more that can be conveyed in a manual. Once you understand the principals of ropework and protecting the leader, proficiency is a matter of practice, and depends to a great extent on common sense and developing an eye for good nut slots – a hopeless task to try to get across in print. Also, yesterday's trick gear is already passé. So, while the physical act of climbing remains basically the same, keeping abreast of current gear and ropework tricks is an ongoing job. Read the magazines and equipment catalogs, and keep your eyes and ears peeled for the latest developments.

Anyway, all the chapters will be broken down along the aforementioned lines: The physical, the mental and the strategic.

Lastly, climbers who have contributed to this manual have in some instances said the same thing I've already stated in so many words. Though we run the risk of repeating ourselves, we benefit by having the salient points driven home again and again.

Slab Climbing

Face climbs that are less than vertical receive little press. The difficulty numbers aren't as high as those on the modern, steeper routes, so the relative prestige is low. But for the majority of recreational climbers, slab routes remain popular. Fabulously pure slab climbing can be found in areas from New Hampshire, North Carolina, Colorado, to California. Most all world-class face climbers are very experienced in slab climbing as well. You must crawl before you walk, and most climbers learn face climbing on slabs. Slabs remain the best medium on which to hone general technique, particularly footwork. They also are excellent for mental conditioning. While the big-name routes might ascend 110° walls, they probably also sport bolt protection every 10 feet. No so with slab climbs, where 50-foot falls are not unheard of. Lastly, many of the modern, steep routes have at least short sections of less-than-vertical face climbing, so by necessity, every seasoned face climber is 'slab fluent.'

BODY POSITION

Good balance is a climber's way of fighting gravity. For the slab climber, good balance primarily is the result of assuming correct body position. On climbs less than about 85° – or just under vertical – you generally want to keep the torso at the same angle you would when walking – straight up and down, remaining 'in balance.' Even the clumsiest man to ever shuffle around in boot leather walks with all of his mass centered directly over his feet. Try balancing a stick on your finger. Should the stick wobble even a centimeter off plum vertical, it topples off. And unless you're walking into a blinding headwind, you can't lean but a few degrees forward without falling. Likewise, unless you've got wings, or Super Glue™ on your boots, you'll slide straight off the stone – straight down – unless you maintain this upright body position.

A vertical torso forces your weight straight onto your boots, and that's essential to gain maximum purchase. The entire point on climbs that are less than vertical is to get your boots to do the work. The arms, regardless of girth or wattage, quickly fizzle out, so keep the torso upright and let the legs labor. Fight the initial urge to

hug the rock. That only directs your mass onto your boots at an oblique angle, forcing you to overcling with your hands in an attempt to compensate for the bogus balance and ever-slipping boots.

Relax

Chinese philosopher Li Fong Chu said the rigid mind is the poor mind. I never quite knew what the hell Fong meant by this, but the rigid climber is certainly the poor climber. Each move produces subtle changes in equilibrium. Providing you keep the torso upright, your body will naturally make all the little adjustments, provided you stay relaxed. No need to go too deeply into this, but a couple tricks are useful. Watch your breathing. When a climber gets scared, or tenses up for whatever reason, the abdominal muscles often tighten, depressing the diaphragm, and breathing comes in little pants. When that happens the climber looks, and probably is, frantic. By breathing regularly, you can fool your otherwise terrified mind and body into relaxing. So always try and breath like you move – fluidly.

No no! Leaning in to the rock to reach those seductive handholds (above) undermines your efforts as much as hugging the rock (below)

Even the really hard less-than-vertical routes are more tenuous than strenuous. So pace yourself. If the going is rugged, move over it quickly, but not hastily. When the climbing eases, slow down. Never dally, but never climb so fast that you needlessly tire yourself. Your overall condition and the climbing at hand will dictate your ideal pace. Regardless of your fitness, you always want to climb using the least amount of strength and energy, and you can do so only when you're relaxed.

As with any sport, little separates the good athlete from the legendary. Many times it's just the latter's ability to concentrate a little better, which is, more times than not, the consequence of a relaxed body and mind. More on this later.

Correct body position and the ability to relax are absolutely fundamental to good slab climbing. That understood, let's talk particulars.

FOOTWORK

They call him the "Master," and if you ever saw him float up a steep slab or dreadful edging problem, you'd know why. Darrell Hensel simply is the best I've ever seen on face climbs that are less than vertical. His arms are like pool cues, so his prowess comes not from raw power but from his uncanny ability to stand on the merest nothing as though it were a footstool. The point is: Maximize use of all footholds. The ability to do so is key to success on face climbs of all angles – from slabs to overhanging test pieces.

Friction

The tires on a dragster are wide because the more rubber there is on the track, the better the 'slicks' grab. Usually, the more of a boot's surface area you can apply to the rock, the better purchase you have. Note that as your heel rises and your weight moves onto your toes, less and less of the boot's sole remains in contact with the rock. Hence, you often will see climbers keeping their heels fairly low in an attempt to get a little more rubber onto the rock – just the opposite of the technique used on difficult edging. In addition, conscious pressing of the toes within the boot will force more toe rubber onto the rock.

How you place your foot is as important as anything else. Wretched form is to ignore this altogether and simply bicycle your feet up the rock. You need not look far to see this in practice – and to see how futile it is. The opposite extreme is to observe some rube performing all manner of superfluous, flashy foot movements and looking like a ballerina. If you want to dance, hit the hardwood, Francois. For slab climbing, think about precision and economy of movement. And pay close attention to how you place your feet.

A little experience will tell you what works best, and where. It's mainly instinctual. Yet it's surprising how many climbers pay little attention to this all important detail – precise footwork. There are many climbers out there who would be world-class, or damn close to it, if their footwork was up to snuff.

Shrewd Boot Placement

Where you place your foot is as important as how you place it. Even glacier-polished and seemingly uniform slabs have irregularities – bumps, ridges, wee shelves, rougher-textured sections. So, to a great extent, the able friction climber is the one who scours the face for footholds, then uses the best ones – with precision. The slightest roughness can make a huge difference in how well, or poorly, your boot will stick. So keep your eyes peeled for any sort of hold or irregularity, however marginal, and place that boot as the gem cutter strikes the ruby – precisely.

Keep much of your focus on your foot placements

Walking on Egg Shells

Extreme friction climbing resembles walking on egg shells – or trying to. The handholds are not there, so deft movement from one foot hold to the next is crucial. In so doing, you are transferring all your weight onto what often are very marginal holds. Avoid jerky moves, and never jump onto holds, as this loads them unnecessarily. Ease onto holds. Extend your leg, and as you press out on the hold, do so fluidly, applying even pressure. As with the dragster, if you power-load the hold, – or simply 'drop the clutch' – the tires, per se, will spin out. Jumping onto a friction hold is the surest way to blow right off of it.

Pure Sole

Keep your boots clean – the soles, anyway. The vast majority of modern 'sticky rubber' rock soles are not rubber at all, but a petroleum-based synthetic (TDR, or thermo-dynamic rubber), which is a magnet for grease, pine sap, etc. Don't hike about in your $125 boots. Carry a toothbrush-sized wire brush in your pack, and spend thirty seconds before a climb giving your soles the once over. No need to submit your boots to Clorox ablutions, resins, emery boards, et. al. A couple passes with the wire brush (water also works) and your boots will perform like they're supposed to.

Pace

Nine times out of 10 you'll want to climb a friction problem in a slow and steady manner. But this is not always the case. Let different conditions dictate pace. For instance, where the rock is extremely polished, the holds are 'time-bomb,' meaning you can stay on them only briefly because your boot starts to butter off the second you weight it. Cat-like agility and a bit of magic (and experience) are your best tools on really greasy and/or tenuous friction holds.

ONE MORE TIME

Again, and probably more so than with any other type of climbing, correct body position is essential for friction climbing. Think of it this way: When an apple falls off a tree, it plummets straight down, demonstrating that gravity is a force driving things straight down – like an arrow loosed from On High that sticks into level ground at a 90-degree angle. For the most part, you'll want to keep your body at this up and down attitude, for it puts your weight directly onto your boots, resulting in maximum friction. Lean in or out from the rock, and the friction decreases dramatically.

A good exercise is to try and climb easy slabs with no hands. It takes but a couple moves to realize all there is to know about body position. I repeat this only because poor body position is so common on slab climbs. Good body position and careful footwork are at least 90 percent of successful frictioning.

Let's step aside for a moment and listen to Bob Gaines, director of Vertical Adventures climbing school. Bob is a wizard on the slabs, and both his vast experience and 10 years of instructing have given him valuable insights. The following is excerpted from his fine treatise, *Slab Talk*:

Practice your balance and poise on easy boulder slabs

"When I began rock climbing in the early 70s, the infamous 'Stonemasters' ruled the Southern California crags. At that time, American and British climbers were setting the standards, and the Stonemasters were doing some of the hardest rock climbs in the world. Entrance into their elite clique was direct: You had to flash Valhalla, a 3-pitch face route at Suicide Rock, perhaps the first 5.11 edging climb in America. Back then, the best shoes were hard-rubber P.A.s and R.D.s, both totally unsuitable for difficult edging and smearing routes like Valhalla. Not until E.B.s came along did the ranks of the Stonemasters grow, though slightly.

"Everything changed when sticky rubber soles arrived. Precise edging was out and smearing was in – pasting the ball of the foot directly onto the rock, letting the edge, crystal or merest rugosity 'bite' into the boot sole. Some climbers referred to this new technique as 'smedging.' Soon, even stickier rubbers appeared, and a slab renaissance ensued. Climbers ventured onto even blanker and steeper slabs. Some of the old test pieces were a full grade easier in the new boots, and by 1985, most every Suicide climber was a Stonemaster. Such is the part technology has played in slab climbing.

"Extreme slab climbing requires quick thinking to unravel puzzling move combinations. Exacting footwork is essential, as is balance and relaxation under duress. Even the slightest quaking will send the boot skating away.

"I like to work in two sets: handholds and footholds. First, I scan the rock for the two best handholds. On edges, I prefer the 'crimp' (placing the thumb over the forefinger) for optimal power. Digging the finger pads straight down onto the hold means positive purchase. When no obvious edges exist, simply digging the pads into the most roughly textured area will help. Many of the most extreme slab cruxes consist of sidepull combinations, pulling sideways on vertical edges with arms extended in an iron-cross position. On low-angle slabs, palming helps keep the center of gravity over the feet. The idea is – 'nose over toes.' Novices are best taught the

Smearing:
The technique of standing on rounded holds.

Palming:
As opposed to grabbing a hold with your fingers, use the friction of your open palm on any hold, bump, shallow etc. that will work.

fundamentals of footwork and balance on low-angle slabs bereft of any handholds, forcing them to trust the friction of their boots while learning the subtleties of body position and center of gravity. Always visually follow the boot all the way to its placement on the hold. Never look up for a handhold until both feet are set. Watch a world-class climber and the first thing you'll notice is the fluid, ultra-precise footwork. Edges, sharp crystals and protruding rugosities are the most obvious smearing targets. On traverses, crossing inside with the opposite foot works best, using the outside portion of the boot that's crossing through to smear with. Ankle flexion helps maintain maximum surface contact between boot sole and rock. Always focus on shifting the center of gravity to directly above the ball of the foot you're stepping up on.

Smearing the soles of the boot over small crystals and into shallow pockets, coupled with an upright posture, is a formula for success on the slabs.

"On extreme slabs, where only the slightest dimples or ripples mar the slab plane, frontpointing on microsmears is called for. Here, just the very front tip of the boot is smeared, with the heel held relatively high. Temperature is key. Modern boot soles smear best at between 45 to 55° Fahrenheit, so take on that nasty pitch in the cool shade. Keep your boot soles meticulously clean. Rub off any dirt and grime and wash the soles if necessary (some climbers use rubbing alcohol to clean their soles). Once shod, never walk around in the dirt. The soles are never the same once dirt-impregnated. And never put chalk on your boot soles, as it greatly reduces your traction.

"The aspiring ace can benefit greatly from a long apprenticeship on the slabs. The subtle tricks of balance and footwork, well-learned through time on the rock, can be applied later to steeper test pieces where footwork still is key to success.

"For the expert, the extreme slab challenge demands a quick mind to solve the puzzle, mental poise and steady resolve for the long runouts, plus the exacting footwork and the balance of a dancer. Success at climbing what looks impossibly blank might just be the sweetest victory of all."

Rick Accomazzo is acknowledged as a master face climber and always has been particularly shrewd on the slabs. Legendary for his composure in the face of chilling runouts, Rick climbs the blankest routes as though he were climbing stairs. In summary, let's find out why. Talk to us, Ricky:

(opposite)
Bob Gaines on "The Hall of Mirrors," Yosemite

Jay Smith photo

"Slab climbing is the most subtle form of face climbing. At relatively low angles (roughly 45 to 70 degrees), difficult climbs make use of minute holds and fine variations in rock texture. It is this subtlety that provides one of the pleasures

of climbing slabs. When you are climbing well, you can amaze yourself by moving over holds that are hardly perceptible. My first climbs were the slab routes of Tahquitz and Suicide Rocks in California, and I still have a fondness for this type of climbing. Let me now pass on some advice gleaned from 19 years experience on slabs, experience gained from trial and error (i.e. by falling often).

"Good footwork is 75 percent of successful slab climbing. Because of the lesser angle, you can afford to be more deliberate than if you are racing against depletion of forearm reserves – which occurs on steeper faces – and you need to be deliberate, for the footing is rarely positive, more often leaning toward the remarkably marginal. It's a contemplative sort of climbing that rewards finesse and balance rather than brute strength and endurance. Since falls are slower than on the vertical, and solid bolt protection often is used, runouts exceeding 20 feet are common. Consequently, to climb slabs well, one must have the ability and confidence to make marginal moves a long way out from the protection. For this, there is no secret: Practice is the only method by which climbers can become proficient and comfortable in the face of long falls. I can offer this tip: It is a natural tendency to tighten up and forget to breathe regularly when the last protection is receding at a disturbing pace and one becomes more and more aware of a long plunge. When I find my heart fluttering and my focus drifting to that last bolt, I stop, take a few slow breaths and try to marshal all my attention to the move at hand. I also make sure my center of gravity is away from the rock; that I have not unconsciously started leaning in, which is a sure prescription for a fall.

"It is more likely that your legs will tire and cause a misstep rather than your arms fatiguing, resulting in a failed grip. Thus, finding a periodic resting place for your feet is essential. Try to give your calves a break by standing on the outside edge of your boot, preferably on a good hold. A few moments on the outside edge can restore feeling to a numbed foot crammed into a snug boot. An even better respite is afforded by finding a hold big enough to stand on using the inside edge of the heel. This takes the pressure off the toes and the confidence tends to return with the blood flow. With practice, you can heel edge on fairly small holds and get a rest even in the midst of considerable difficulties.

"You must be in a good position to scrutinize the rock for the tiny slab nuances that can serve as holds. When looking down for potential footholds, it often helps to get your eyes close to the rock. From this attitude, you can see small differences in gradient or slight depressions or bumps that might offer purchase for your rock shoes. With your eyes close to the rock, the surface does not look nearly as featureless and flat, and you instantly become aware of more options than even a studied, straight-on look would afford.

"You must keep your weight over your feet. That is essential. The body (particularly the arse) must be kept as far as possible from the rock. This centers the weight over the feet and onto the shoes, ensuring maximum friction. Unfortunately, this position makes long reaches for handholds all the more perilous. As you reach, the hips draw closer to the rock and just as you attain that blue-ribbon nubbin, your feet will glide off, and down you go. I have seen many experienced climbers fall into this dilemma, which probably is the most common cause for slab falls. Better to make an intermediate step up, even if questionable, rather than try for that long reach.

"So, how do you keep your hips away from the rock, maintain the proper body position and still getting a good look at potential footholds? Simply bend *at the waist,* place the top of your head against the rock and peer down from this position. The attitude forces the hips out and keeps maximum weight on the feet, while at the same time allowing a prime angle for spying footholds. While not the most dignified posture, it works wonderfully."

Note: Because friction and edging routes have so many similarities, we will review strategy for both modes at the end of the following section on edging.

Bullseye Edging

Propitious boot placement – the ability to place the boot precisely on the hold – comes with experience. And everyone does things a little differently; hence, there are no rules stating how to stand on this or that hold. There are, however, various concepts that most climbers follow to get the best placement.

Because of the foot's biomechanics, the available stability of your toes when crammed into a skin-tight boot and the natural position your foot assumes when placed on a hold, climbers generally do most of their edging with the big toe, right where the nail cuts back. This 'great toe' posture is pretty much the standard edging position on perhaps 70 to 80 percent of all edging moves. There are exceptions, though. Mari Gingery, one of America's premier face climbers, normally edges using the ball of her foot (ball edging), weighting several inches back from her big toe. If anything, this position is even stronger than the great toe position, but most climbers go with the latter because of the increased sensitivity of the toe.

The able edger, however, can edge with any part of his boot – even the heel – because there are many situations where the hold is not clear cut or dead horizontal. On these obscure holds, the great toe position may be inferior to using the point of the boot, the side, or anything else that will work. The position of the edge, relative to your body position, determines what part of the boot you will edge with. The general idea is to edge wherever it feels most natural. If you are not confident edging with anything but the great toe, you will have to crook your ankle in all sorts of funky attitudes to hold the edge. You can go only so far using the single edge, so get accustomed to using whatever part of the boot the move or climb requires.

Using the point of the boot is useful and necessary for pockets, and sometimes for very small edges. It also comes into play on big edges (explained later). If your feet are unusually strong, the heel can be kept low, but most climbers hinge the heel up slightly when 'point' edging. Unless the edge is down-sloping, the heel most always is

(opposite)
Ron Kauk at Nimes, France

Beth Wald photo

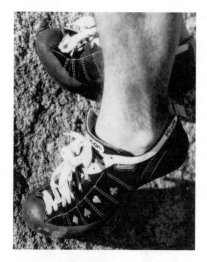

higher than the toe. Learning to edge with the outside of the boot is a trick that few climbers ever master, but it pays high dividends to those that do. It is particularly useful when the legs are splayed far apart and you need to back-step an edge to match, or exchange, feet and step through. Also, the move is useful when you're cranked to the side, with one hip on, or near, the rock. Your ability to use the outside edge of your inside boot is a must here. Practice on boulders. It's an invaluable trick. It's also effective as a method to rest tired feet on holds that otherwise would pump your calves even worse.

Steady As You Go

Perhaps the most important aspect of good edging is the ability to maintain a stable boot on the hold. That is, once you have precisely placed the boot, you must maintain the exact boot posture as you step up and eventually put your full weight on the edge. On occasion, your heel may have to move, say, to hinge up for a high reach; but the attitude of the boot's running edge on the foothold must not change. This is a very tricky technique, and usually takes some years to master.

Another word about placement: Once you select the edge, weight it momentarily and make the necessary micro-adjustments until it is in the optimum position. This is principally a matter of feel, of jockeying the boot around till it feels most secure. When a boot blows off an edge, it is most often a case of the boot's running edge moving ever so slightly on the foothold and rotating off. The smaller the hold, the more important that the boot's running edge remain immobile once weighted.

Smearing

Good smearing often is a matter of strong toes. Normally, you smear by lightly overlapping the hold with the boot's running edge. Since 1980, and the introduction of the 'sticky' rubber soles, many old edging problems now are readily smeared. No need to elaborate much here. The same techniques hold as with edging: shrewd choice of footholds, fluid weighting of the holds, and good body position only increase your smearing prowess.

Horrendous Edging

Once the angle nears 75 degrees, you have to have something decent to hold onto or you're not going very far.

But what is 'decent?' Unfortunately, anything. If the wall is pretty smooth, you'll be pulling on edges – hopefully edges that are big and plentiful. They rarely are, however. And when they are sparse, small and razor-sharp, you're talking 'Horrendous Edging' – a dreadful mix of cranking your brains out while staying balanced on extremely tenuous holds, enduring extreme muscular tension and maintaining controlled relaxation. It sounds pretty pedantic, but that's what you're looking at. Such climbing is usually found on granite domes.

Whereas slab climbing is a matter of balance, footwork and finesse, steep edging entails strength, precise footwork and the ability to quickly figure out and execute obscure moves. First, handholds.

GRAB IT

There are, of course, the 'open,' the 'cling,' and the 'vertical' grips, one of which is used on virtually all edging climbs. (We'll take up 'pocket' and 'pinch' grips later.) The open and vertical grips are pretty self-explanatory, and are used infrequently on edging problems (particularly the open grip, which is used mainly on larger, rounded holds). So the cling grip has emerged as the principal mode. Getting familiar with the cling grip on lower-angled climbs is one thing; but once you really start heaving on small edges, the cling grip takes some getting used to. There are no rare tricks to make things easier; the surest, and quickest way to master the cling grip is on the boulders. When you start loading your fingers with full body weight, the joints will smart something terrible, particularly at the bent (second) knuckle. But the digits quickly get accustomed to the strain. By 'crimping' – wrapping your thumb over your index finger – you can increase the power of your grip substantially. Aside from things that you eventually will learn on your own . . .

Consider the following points:

'Contact' strength is the amount of torque you can apply to a given hold. It's everything in edging, and can vary dramatically according to how your fingers are placed on an edge. So, the first and foremost concern is to grab the hold in the best spot, i.e., where you can apply the most crank.

Experience is the key here, yet it's amazing how many experienced climbers show little skill in precise hand placement. They simply grab the hold willy nilly, then pull. Wrong. Any edge, however uniform, affords a 'best' position for your fingertips, which is all you'll be using on horrendous edging routes. Remember that your index and second finger are far stronger than your ring finger and pinky. Try to get the former two digits well set on the best and sharpest part of the edge. It's a simple and almost instantaneous procedure. You eyeball the edge, place your hand on it and before cranking, simply dance your fingers over it for a split second. There are so many nerves in your fingertips that

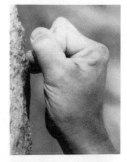

From the top: the open, cling and vertical grips, each employing the thumb for added power and purchase.

finding the section of the edge where your fingers are most secure is very easy. By applying a little torque to the hold, you quickly can verify your grip, or jockey your fingers slightly to improve it. It all takes seconds once you've got some practice; and seconds, even split-seconds, is all you'll want to spend tinkering with it. It might be all you'll have.

Your strongest digit is your thumb – by far. So whenever possible, wrap your thumb over the nail of your index finger and enjoy at least a twenty-percent boost in cranking might. This 'crimping' technique is essential for hard edging, and takes but a few hours to get used to. After several climbs, the thumb will automatically wrap over the index finger, and pulling on small holds will feel strange and imbalanced otherwise.

The 'vertical' grip, which involves pulling straight down on the edge, is simply too painful to be used much. It can pry the fingernails far enough back to slide a bamboo shoot into the breech. But now, as climbers increasingly are suffering Auschwitz-type diets hoping to shed that last gram of blubber, the vertical grip may be gaining popularity. I doubt it, though. At over two-hundred pounds, I can count on one hand the times I've used the vertical grip (and it never worked for me – not once). But there are no rules, and if you think the vertical grip will work, grimace and go with it. Fingernails do grow back . . . .

Lastly, whatever grip you use, try to get the heel of the palm well-seated on the rock. This can get you additional purchase, via friction between palm to rock, but is not always possible. If it feels unnatural to bend your wrist in to get your palm on the rock, forget it. If it does feel okay, though, it's a boon.

Rosy Palms

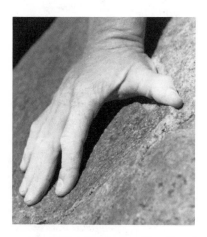

It is useful to position fingers of the palmed hand on edges or depressions

On slabs and lower-angled edging routes, the features need not be large or well-defined to help our cause. This is particularly so with various palming maneuvers, where the hand is placed flat over, or against, an irregularity – a bump, wee shelf, or any roughly-textured spot often will do. When the angle is quite low, you actually can mantel off a well-placed palm, usually positioned with the fingers pointing straight down. More common is a lateral palm, where you press or lean off the palm for balance. Sometimes opposing palms can afford enough purchase, if only briefly, to move the feet up. The most useful, and common palm, is the one placed in a mantel position, while the other hand pulls on an edge. In most instances, both the edge and the palm are very marginal, and the move requires consummate balance, plus the ability to weight both holds just short of the point that they will skid off. On the truly grim cruxes, it's a case of all four limbs being poised on

borderline holds. Oftentimes, the palm is the best of the four. In the absence of any edges to palm off, simply pressing the fingers of the palmed hand into tip-sized depressions is enough to stop the hand from skidding off.

Chalking for any of these palming moves is an art. Remember that it's the friction of the fingers and heel of the palm that provides the grab, and that too much chalk can actually reduce that friction. Use just enough to keep the palm dry, but not so much that you have a slippery layer between the palm and the doubtlessly poor hold.

Palm below to stabilize your body on the slab and to walk your feet up a slab.

WATCH ME . . . I'M MANTELING!

On slabs, quasi-manteling – palming off shelves, bumps, or any feature – is common. But once the angle steepens even

Place your hands carefully on a mantel hold to maximize their purchasing power.

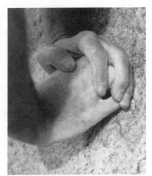

Manteling

slightly, mantels should be avoided if possible. You often can face climb around a mantelshelf. You don't want to end up totally pressed out on some unctuous bump, with no handhold to grab above and no way to stand on said bump. Always assume that once initiated, you cannot reverse the mantel, since most of the time you cannot. If you must mantel, do this first: Scan the face above the mantelshelf and note any handhold you can grab once you have pressed out the mantel. Do not crank the mantel and hope there is a hold above to grab. Invariably, there will be nothing there. Secondly, spot the hold on which you will place your toe once you have pressed out the mantel. With a good handhold above, this may be the mantel hold itself. Select the best part of the hold to mantel on. Sometimes this will not be the most clear-cut spot, rather a roughly-textured section where the heel of your palm can get good bite. If there's no hold above to grab once you've pressed out the mantel, remember you must leave enough of the mantelshelf exposed to place a boot on. Here, you press your body high enough to set that toe on the mantled hold, then gently rock all your weight over the hold and gingerly stand up. The key here is extending the leg, which can be very strenuous. A common mistake is to 'power-load' the hold, applying too much pressure too soon. The toe – which often is marginally set – can blow off the hold. A slow, fluid leg extension is usually the ticket.

Most mantels are done with the heel of the palm. You also can mantel off your fingertips, if strength and angle allow, and this is actually a better position to be in for the moves that will follow. It's often much more taxing, however. Again, try to avoid the mantel if at all possible, unless doing so is far harder than cranking it out.

BODY MECHANICS

Arm Position

There are several things concerning arm movement and position that we will exhaust in the chapter on vertical face climbing. For now, let's briefly review the basics.

Because slab and edging routes are lower-angled than other types of climbs, arm position is not so crucial in terms of saving strength. Most of your weight is over your feet, or should be. Arm position does effect your balance, however. The best posture is when your body is in a sort of relaxed X. That means both arms should be grabbing holds above your head. Obviously, the climb dictates exactly where your hands must go, and you'll routinely pull this way or that, with your hands to the side or even below your chest. Just remember that you are in better balance, and in a more natural posture to both stand and pull, when your hands are over your head and about shoulders' width apart. Strive to work with your arms in this position whenever possible.

You'll sometimes see climbers that appear to be clinging to the rock for their lives, with their hands perpetually at chest or shoulder-level – belt-level, even. It's very hard to stay relaxed, in balance and also avoid overclinging in this posture. Sometimes you have to assume a different position – for instance, if the holds are widely spaced – but among

The relaxed X position; climbers at Verdon Gorge, France

Bob Gaines photo

other detriments, it blocks your downward vision, making it hard to zero in on footholds.

Legs

Ideally, you'll want to keep your legs extended, slightly bent, with the heels in so you can edge with the great toe. Moving from one foothold to the next should involve small, unexaggerated steps – as though you were climbing a ladder, one rung at a time. Of course, most every climb has a bunch of high steps as well. Generally, the higher the step, the harder it is to press out, the trickier the balance is and the more weight is placed on the hold – and all this means your foot can blow off the hold a lot easier than if you were making smaller moves. When you've a choice, make two smaller moves rather than one long one. This is particularly important to those just getting acquainted with hard face climbing. Keep making unnecessary high steps and soon the dreaded 'sewing-machine leg' will kick in, where your legs start quaking like you're climbing toward the electric chair. Stick with the smaller moves whenever possible. Less work, better balance – better climbing all around.

Torque Wrench

The best wicked edgers always appear relaxed. They seem not to be working hard, though their fingers and toes hurt like everyone else's. They understand the difference between staying tight on the holds, and climbing rigid, or frozen. Much of their poise comes from knowing just how hard, or how little, to pull. Overclinging is the quickest way to fatigue and fall. Every move is not the crux – not on any climb. You don't use a sledge hammer to sink a thumb tack, nor do you use a tack hammer on railroad spikes. Knowing how to use just the right amount of torque on a hold only comes with experience, but so long as you understand the principle, you're halfway to the belay.

STRATEGY

On most any face climb, you can conceive a workable strategy by eyeballing the pitch. That's because vertical climbs have features (lest you'd never be able to climb them), so you can see what you are up against. Not so on slab and edging routes, where the climb is nigh featureless, and leaders have a hard time seeing holds that are right in front of their faces. Only so much can be learned from a visual inspection. So our strategy, to a great extent, must be drawn from other sources. Also, there are considerations other than cranking the actual moves that should be factored into the equation.

Shrewd Counsel

If we agree that a good strategy is that which prepares a climber for the lead, then why not quiz everyone you know who has climbed a certain route? Find out all you can – what the climb entails, what are the moves and protection like, where is the crux, etc. Some climbers are too proud to ask around and get the 'beta.' They're the ones whose ears are peeled back when someone else is describing a route they intend to do. Be warned, however, that what you hear from one source is bound to differ from a second source. Best to get a stack of opinions. From them all, you usually can draw a useful, general picture of the climb. Guidebook topos are useful for generic information and tend to be more objective. But many times it's these subjective, first-hand accounts that give you the best 'vibes' about what to expect.

BATTING PRACTICE

The value of experience cannot be overstated. If you have climbed quite a few 5.9 climbs, for example, another 5.9 route, while perhaps challenging, should not surprise you with its technical difficulties. You know you're up for the task, which bolsters the confidence. And never underestimate the importance of climbing easier routes as well. When you're on easier ground, you can relax far more than when you're pressed. Climbing easy routes is like a baseball player taking batting practice. Think of the Yankee centerfielder, who takes hours of batting practice every week. The batting-practice pitcher just lobs the ball over the plate – it's like a 5.2 climb for a 5.9 climber – but the hitter can fully concentrate on the mechanics of his swing because the situation is much more controlled. If he faces only game-speed pitching, if he's always pressed to his maximum, he'll eventually loose form and slump. This is one of the problems facing the hotshot whose only interest is in scaling the hardest routes. If he sticks just to the bleak stuff – the 'live pitching,' if you will – his technique will improve slower than if he were to spend some time every outing doing easier climbs, settling into a comfortable flow and rhythm, and experiencing the mastery of climbing something flawlessly. It's like hammering meatballs over the fence, and feeling like The Bambino in doing so.

Bouldering

Hard bouldering is the best practice for cranking difficult edging cruxes. You always can do harder moves on boulders than you can on a rope, because you can try them ad nauseum. Moreover, if you do enough hard-edging bouldering problems, you will have executed, in one fashion or another, most every conceivable sequence. This helps you recognize similar sequences on any nasty route. It's amazing how many times you can cross-reference the route at hand with other climbs or boulder sequences. From your mental logbook, you can call up moves that worked before, and probably will work again. And whatever you run up against, it's most likely going to be easier, probably far easier, than what you have already cranked on the boulders. Bouldering is your best advisor, a proven method to build strength, technique and confidence. More on bouldering later.

Razors Rip My Flesh

You only have so many razor cranks in you at a given time. That is, your fingertips wear out before your muscles do. Edges usually are very sharp and can cut to the quick. You'll want to build up those callouses, either on the boulders or by doing hard edging routes – preferably, by doing both. One famous climber draws a bastard-file over his fingertips during off-days, but I cannot endorse this method.

No matter how tough your fingertips are, a hard, sustained edging route can shred them. The most common gash is a 'split tip,' where the skin parts in frown-like fashion along the thin arcing line of a fingerprint. These are painful, and take up to two weeks to fully heal. Attempts to Crazy-Glue™ split tips back together have been somewhat

Craig Smith on
"Darkness at Noon," a
5.13a at Smith Rock

Beth Wald photo

successful, but this is a stopgap measure that only leads to more serious injury. Once you cut through to the dermis, the genuine meat, you'd best lay off for a while. Or go with cracks for a spell.

You want to climb a given route taking as few falls as possible, because that will preclude you from having to repeat hard, painful moves and cut your fingers all the more – one more reason to work up a good strategy before tackling the lead.

There are probably more falls logged on steep edging routes than on any other type of climbing. Because these routes tend to be both steep and smooth, even minor injuries are rare (but not that rare). This is an advantage, because concentration must be absolutely focused, not worried about the consequences of a fall. And when a fall is even remotely possible, you must know how to appraise the situation to emerge unscathed.

Harrowing Runout

The stamp of the classic slab and/or edging climb often is the shiver-me-timbers runout. Perhaps climbers traditionally have tried to run the rope on these routes because the falls are often – though not always – more skids than true plunges. Whatever the reasons, the technical rating of a slab or edging climb often is secondary to the relative protection of the lead – or the lack of protection, as it were. Mind you, all slab or edging climbs are not runout – not by any means. But there are more than a few that feature potential falls of 50 feet. On rare occasions, entire pitches have no protection whatsoever. Obviously, these climbs are not for everybody. They were designed for and are scaled by folk who climb for reasons other than mere 'recreation.' Anyway, since experienced climbers approach all runouts the same way – be the runout 10 or 50 feet in length – we can discuss things in general terms.

Shall I?

The first decision you must make is whether or not you're even interested in climbing a potentially dangerous route. And make no mistake about it – just because the route is not real steep *does not* mean a 25-foot fall, for instance, is harmless. Any fall can hurt you. If you decide to have a look at a runout climb, do so with an open mind. If you don't like the looks of it, don't let pride, or a pushy partner, commit you.

Once you reach the belay below the runout pitch, study the rock closely. If you decide to have a go, keep your options open. If you get to the runout and, for whatever reason, don't feel like casting off, bail the hell off. There's always another day. If you still feel like having a go, *think through the consequences!!* The tried and true method is to understand a simple formula entailing three key considerations: How long is the longest possible fall you can take? Estimate the potential and judge how far below the protection you will end up. Is the protection adequate to hold such a fall? And most importantly, what, if anything, will you hit if you come off? Don't underestimate even the slightest feature. A small ripple or horn can catch an ankle and ruin your day. Know what and where any hazards are. Note that only the last of these queries is a true judgement call – will the protection hold? The length of the fall and the obstacles along the way can be visually determined. In a nutshell, answering these questions is the surest way to calculate the potential risk of any fall, regardless of whether the route is 5.0 or 5.14. If everything checks out, then you've got to put all doubts out of your mind and really go after it. Fear paralyzes power, saps resolve and makes relaxing virtually impossible. If the potential fall does not appear to have dire consequences, but you're still petrified, better not to cast off.

Unruffled

The key to climbing any runout is to stay calm and climb with absolute control. Try to stick with conservative, straightforward sequences, even if they require more strength to execute. Many legendary falls happen when the climber has a moment's lapse in concentration, tries an unusual, weird move, or gets rattled towards the end of the runout and simply defeats himself.

Not all runouts are hazardous – they have the potential, yes, but if you're a 5.8 climber and the runout is only 5.5, you've got it made if you can simply 'keep the lid on.'

The really risky runout is something all serious climbers will face somewhere, sometime. The possible scenarios are countless, but the bottom line is the same: You fall, you get hurt. Perhaps the protection is poor. Maybe there's no protection. There might be something to hit if you come off – like the ground. Whatever, the degree of risk is relative to how close the climbing is to your technical limit. If the climbing seems relatively easy, and you can keep your head together, the risks are usually, but not always, manageable. If, however, the long unprotected section is near your technical limit, you're playing with fire. There's a fine line separating the bold climber from the blockhead. Good judgement – which cannot be conveyed in a manual – is the call here. Just remember that few climbers get away with cheating injury for very long, and no climber gets away with it forever. Again, think hard before trying a route that is both difficult to protect and is near your technical limit. Technical skill and placing protection are separate arts, and it's *very questionable* to push both points at the same time.

FALLING

Falling is an integral part of slab and edging routes. Many of these routes ascend featureless rock, but are bolt-protected, which eliminates – if the bolts are sound – much of the peril. On routes steeper than about 65 degrees, the falling climber will almost certainly lose contact with the rock and go airborne. A slab fall, however, usually is more of a skid than an honest-to-God, wrenching fall. These factors all encourage a climber to challenge himself. Chance a fall if the consequences aren't too frightening, and don't ignore the consequences: How far can you fall? What will you hit? Will the pro hold the longest possible fall?

Knowing where you are in relation to your protection also is important – very important. If you are directly above the pro, or nearly so, you should fall straight down and it should be uneventful if everything goes right – if the pro holds, if you hit nothing and if you maintain correct body position. When you're off to one side of the protection – either directly to the side, as on a traverse, or above and to the side – things can get nasty in a hurry. But first, let's discuss the straight-down fall:

The most common injuries on slab falls are minor abrasions and barked hips and elbows. Because the rock is comparatively low-angled, your body naturally will grate over the surface unless you make a conscious effort to keep your torso away. Bruised hips occur when the climber gets turned sideways. Thus, there are two things to try to do. When you pop, keep both palms on the rock, arms bent but straight enough to keep your face and chest away from the rock. Keep your feet spread slightly apart and slide down on the soles of your boots. You want to slide down in a four-point stance, staying relaxed, and facing the rock. I've taken 50-foot falls in this posture and come away without a scratch. If you freeze up and get turned sideways, you can injure yourself quickly and unnecessarily. There is no mystery to it. If you stay relaxed and skid down in the four-point stance, you should be okay. Doing so is, to a large degree, a result of pre-programming your mind. A fall happens so fast that, once airborne, you'll only have time to react. If you're pre-programmed to relax and assume the four-point stance, you're doing yourself a favor. If not, expect the worst. (But don't expect to see your life flash before your eyes. That's a load of crap.)

If you are off to one side of the protection, the main worry when falling is that you'll get jerked sideways and spin. This can twirl you like a rag-doll, and you can smack limbs – perhaps even your head – on the rock (though a head-rock collision is rare). Again, you must maintain the four-point stance, trying to bridge, or skid, with at least one limb in the direction you are falling. If, say, you've traversed to the right, then try to absorb the spinning action with your left arm and leg. The right arm should be high and to the right, palming off the rock as you slide sideways, trying to maintain stability as you whip over. There is an art to this, much of which depends on natural agility. A few short falls can be very instructive. As long as you have the theory in your mind, you'll probably be able to perform it well enough. Letting your body skid gently over the rock is much easier than it sounds. Just stay relaxed and maintain the four-point stance.

(opposite)
Kelly Carignan on
"Mickey Mantel",
Suicide Rock, California.

Greg Epperson photo

There's another method on traverse falls that is remarkably effective if you've the athletic ability to pull it off. It entails grabbing the rope just above your tie-in and sort of sprinting along the arc of your fall. This 'Jack-be-nimble' method is not necessary on routes above, say, 70 degrees, where it's easier to just slide across. But when the angle is just right, and the fall is a short one, it works well. Trip up and you're in trouble, however.

Constructive Fall

Many times a climber falls because he was so afraid of falling that he tensed up, climbed hesitantly, or made a hasty move that cost him. If the fall is uneventful, which it normally is, it can do wonders for a person's confidence. Knowing falls can be harmless dispells the jitters and frees the climber to concentrate on the moves. You can rarely climb to your full potential if you are preoccupied with falling. You hear people saying that the only reason they managed the lead was because they were too scared to fall off. This is usually more of a 'war story,' than a true one, however.

Jive Fall

Some climbers actually will jump off cruxes rather than try a difficult move that they think, correctly or not, they will fall off anyway. I suppose some fractured reasoning can justify this, but it seems unsportsmanlike not to push yourself until you pop because of the difficulty, rather than jumping off because you are afraid to try something. When you are climbing with a toprope, there is absolutely no reason not to climb until you fall off. Assuming you actually want to climb the pitch, it's really questionable not to give it an all-out try. How else will you ever learn your limit, or improve? Regardless, you never want to fall, so to do so intentionally seems absurd to me.

Out Of The Blue

Impact Force:
The amount of shock
a body receives at the
end of a fall.

At least half of your falls will occur unexpectedly, usually when a foot pops off the hold. When you climb yourself into a position where you can't move on, warn your belayer. Then go ahead and try the move anyway. You might make it, and you're no worse off if you don't.

After a fall of more than 20 feet, the rope suffers appreciable fiber elongation and structural deformation, most of which is recovered with time. So, after any longish fall, lower down to the belay, tie yourself in with a sling, and untie from the rope for at least 10 minutes. The knot absorbs upwards of 30 percent of the impact force, but will recover quickly once untied.

Lastly, all of these techniques have been mentioned to help reduce the chance of injury if and when you fall. Only a rascal would encourage someone to go fall off something. You never want to fall, no matter how harmless things may appear. But to always climb scared and never to push yourself for fear of falling is a very outdated approach to climbing. More conservative tactics once were essential – when hempen ropes routinely snapped and the pitons were malleable iron. Times have changed.

A FEW TRICKS

This is not the venue to discuss protection in any great, or even moderate, detail; but a couple tricks are worth mentioning. Rope drag is the curse of all slab climbs. Because of the relatively low angle of the rock, the simple motion of the cord running over the stone creates considerable drag on a pitch of any length. Use runners and quickdraws to reduce this drag, and to keep the rope running in as straight a line as possible.

Sew It Up?

Because your body skids over the rock in a slab fall, this kind of fall generates considerably less impact force on protection than a fall on steeper routes. Thus, even marginal nuts can arrest a fall. If your only option for pro is a nut that would never hold a fall on vertical terrain, place it anyway. Many times 'psychological' protection – nuts that appear nearly worthless –

> ### To reiterate . . . .
> - Maintain good body position.
> - Use precise footwork.
> - Keep a relaxed but steady pace.
> - Scope the route and the topo prior to casting off.
> - Develop a good strategy calculating run-outs and potential falls.
> - Avoid rope drag.

have held a slab fall. If the nut is poor, but you can get others in at the same place, do so. Load it up. Place three, four, five poor nuts if need be. Equalize them as well as you can and they might just do the job. Even if they do pop, they often can slow your fall considerably.

GAME PLAN

There is a procedure, or ritual, that good climbers go through before a lead. I'll repeat several previous notions, if only to drive them home. On difficult slab and/or edging routes, the protection often is thin and the potential falls often are long ones. So first, study the topo and make mental notes about how hard the route is, where the crux is, and anything else you can glean from the map. Bilk friends or acquaintances of all relevant info – get the 'beta.' Then, eyeball the hell out of the pitch in question and make certain what you see jibes with both the topo and your friend's reports – can you spot the roof, the horn, the tree? Where are the bolts, and above which one is the crux? Calculate the potential falls between protection, or where you imagine they would be should you have to protect the pitch yourself. Arrange your rack according to what the climb dictates. If you see you'll need runners straightaway, have them, or anything else needed, at the ready. Discuss things with your partner. In short, do a detective job from the deck, and get all your ducks in line before you cast off.

On the really bleak routes, consider these three, basic things: Focus, Form and Rhythm.

Focus

Keen focus on the climbing at hand is essential because the holds often are hard to spot and correct sequences can be difficult to decipher. In a way, you can look at a difficult slab route as a complicated musical score that you must sight read and perform – perfectly. You've got to stay focused throughout, and not let anything deter your concentration. Master slab climber Rick Accomazzo was amazing at staying focused. You could have riddled the stone with bullets and never distracted him. The belayer must concentrate as well. He should keep a trained eye on the leader, feathering the line out, ever ready to catch him should he pop. Sloppy belays can add yards to a fall simply because the belayer was caught unawares. Knowing that your belayer has got all his attention focused on you helps free your mind to deal with the climbing, and is a real confidence builder when you've got to run the rope out a ways.

Perfect Form

No matter how grim the climbing gets, you should never abandon your form. Period. And that's not just to appear stylish. If you ever have the chance to accompany a top climber up an extreme route, do it – even if you have to rest on the cord a few times. You don't want to make a career out of this, but everybody's done it at one time. Chances are the ace will fall a few times, if the route is a test piece. You probably will be surprised by the fall, because it will come so unexpectedly. You'll be surprised because, right up till the ace pitched off, he never forsook his form. Trying wild, desperate moves is rarely, if ever, the solution to a difficult crux. Even if a dynamic move is required, control is the key.

When a climber confronts a climb that seems too difficult, the tendency is to start flailing. We've all seen this type of reaction in a boxing match. Often, the boxer is not even over-matched, but for whatever reason, he chucks form out the window and starts throwing wild haymakers. Rarely does such a blow find its mark. So, at all costs – even a fall – maintain your form. Relax, climb smoothly and maintain control. Do not rush. If you can't do it with good form, how can you expect to do it with poor form?

Maintaining perfect form is essential to make any real gains, particularly with climbers just coming into their own. It's an easy thing to think about, but most climbers consciously must try to maintain form until it becomes automatic.

Rhythm

(opposite)
Boone Speed zeros in on the next hold

Kevin Powell photo

Maintaining good form is important for dozens of reasons, and setting a good pace is no less vital. The idea is to settle into a groove, a rhythm, that is neither too fast, nor too slow. As mentioned, the climb and your aptitude (fitness,

disposition, etc.) will in part dictate your pace, but remember this: Once you settle into a nice flow, you don't want to disrupt it with quick bursts or by 'camping' too long, even on big footholds. Certainly, you should take advantage of rest holds, but don't stay so long as to fall out of sync, letting your focus lag, your muscles get cold, and your feet go numb. You're not in a track meet, but you're not up there to dink around, either. Get on with it in a measured, calculated way.

MODUS OPERANDI

We've gone over the ritual of studying the topo, then eyeballing the devil out of the slab, recognizing and making mental notes about where the crux is, etc. Your gear is in order, and now you're set to cast off. How will you go about your business, and what you will have in mind as you climb over different sections? Here is one method that works well.

Say you are a solid 5.9 climber. The next pitch – your lead, incidentally – is rated 5.10–, but that's only the crux, which is short and near the end of the lead. The rest of the climbing is mostly 5.8. You *know* that everything but the crux is within your capabilities. So, in a sense, you can reduce the entire pitch to perhaps 10 feet of grim climbing, because that's how long the crux is. By looking at it this way, you shrink the questionable bit right down to size, and the project seems more reasonable. You also ease doubts and worries, and can settle into a nice flow, getting your body and mind in a rhythm, before you tackle the crux.

Make sure you don't race over the climbing before reaching the crux. Use the lead-up climbing to get in sync, to settle in and hit your groove. Conserve your gusto. That way you'll be ready when the going gets tough. Once there, study the crux if you can, but not so long as to fall out of your groove.

Many slab/edging climbs are difficult not because of a certain hard crux, but because they are tiring and unrelenting. Known variously as 'calf burners,' 'finger shredders,' et. al., they can be intense affairs because of the degree of concentration needed to assail them. Though these types of climbs might not have as high a rating as ones featuring a vicious crux, they often are just as challenging and almost always more work. An edging route rated 5.10a that features no climbing whatsoever under 5.9 is much more troublesome than a route rated 5.10d that is mostly 5.7, save for a couple beastly moves. That's why the ratings on slab and edging climbs can mislead us.

If the climb is continuously grim, bear these points in mind: Good concentration and continuous, fluid movement are essential. There is a tendency to both speed up and tense up as you near the end of the pitch. Avoid both by staying relaxed and focused. Settle in, stay cool and relaxed, and keep moving. Briefly rest at any decent hold. Stand on your heels and take a little pressure off your calves. Shake out your arms, relax your fingers. Then advise your belayer and have at it.

Ten-Tone Psyche

We will take a good look at psychological preparation in the chapter on overhanging face climbing. These difficult overhanging routes require such a Herculean effort to scale that involved psyche-up techniques are invaluable. For now, let's look at one important concept that is as important as any self-hypnosis or imaging rituals. It goes like this: If you're really going to challenge yourself, your best results will come only when you really feel like doing it. That sounds a little fuzzy, but let's take a moment to rack it into focus.

One of the best things about climbing is that it's altogether unofficial. No coaches, no schedule, no prescribed workouts. You climb what you want, when you want. It's inevitable that as you get more involved in the sport, you will set certain goals for yourself. Eventually, you will head for the cliff with a particular route in mind. You'll say, I'm going to meet Shawn at the Sham Rock and we're going to climb Blarney. As a rule, the closer Blarney is to your technical limit, the more unpredictable your success. That's because there really is no telling how you'll feel, physically or mentally, once you get to Sham Rock. You may have psyched yourself up for a week, worked out diligently, consumed tonics and herbs, chanted, got down on your knees and prayed to the good Lord, yet all was for naught because on that particular day, you felt flat – just weren't into it – despite all the preparations. The best-laid plans, and all that. Despite 'common sense,' a spontaneous decision is often the most productive. Let me give you an example.

I had been trying to complete a new route at a local crag for some months, but always got stopped cold at the last crux. I had tried every conceivable approach, even camping at the base, but still – no go. Finally, I gave up. Some months later, I was at the same crag. I had been to a bachelor's party the previous night, and, feeling pretty jaded, went with easy routes in the morning. After a couple hours, I inexplicably started feeling pretty honed and was anxious to turn up the heat. When we walked past the climb that had repeatedly routed me, I simply knew the time was perfect for another go. I couldn't walk by. I *had* to try it right then and there. I felt like I could do it, and that conviction grew into a 'ten-ton psyche.' I hadn't planned on trying the route till that very second. That day, I finally bagged it.

The point is, there is no way to predict when you'll feel like charging the lions. But when you do, realize it and make your move. You often see this phenomenon in track and field. Perhaps lately a runner has not been getting the marks he's expected. Maybe he's not even peaked for the race. Yet for unknown reasons, on a given night, everything comes together for him. He grabs the moment and a record falls. There was no predicting it, as there rarely is with the breaking of records. Most every track athlete performs best in practice. When he tries to predict a world record, how often does he come through? Rarely, if ever. That's because it's impossible for even a world-class athlete to predict how he will feel at a given meet. But with climbing, there need not be a meet for it to count – everything counts. So if you're walking past a route that previously has humbled you, but you presently feel like you've simply got to try it, if you've got the 'ten-ton psyche,' disregard your other plans. Jump on that route then and there. Get it while you're hot.

To summarize, let's listen to some climbers who have shown mastery in both slab and friction climbing. Kevin Powell and Darrell Hensel are at the top of everyone's list; they were doing 5.12 climbs 15 years ago. Says Powell and Hensel:

"Tenuous test pieces and horrendous edging – this type of climbing, usually found on less than vertical rock, is where you will come to know the meaning of minute holds, tenuous positioning and precise execution. First, let's talk about gear.

"Because precise footwork forms the basis of horrendous edging, don't skimp in obtaining the best possible footwear. Important features are harder rubber on the soles, lateral as well as longitudinal stiffness in the toe area and a close, tight fit overall. Any sloppiness in fit will allow the foot to slide and/or rotate inside the boot (during an edging move), greatly diminishing your ability and confidence when standing on minute holds. Experiment with different models on the boulders until you find just the right boot.

"Chalk should be chosen carefully. It should be somewhat coarse, without that 'slick' feeling. Avoid the fine, powdery stuff, and don't even consider colored chalks, which cake the holds, making them noticeably more greasy. In addition, colored chalks do not remove well with a toothbrush. A stiff-bristled toothbrush is essential for cleaning holds and should be located (on the chalk bag) for quick and easy access.

"Other equipment needs will vary according to route and personal preference; what won't vary is the careful and calculated way in which you organize the gear. Rack up so you can easily and quickly access the gear with a minimum of fiddling in dicey situations. Remember, even the slightest annoyance or distraction can divert you from your goal.

"The techniques and intricacies of horrendous edging, though not easily mastered, can best be learned on the boulders. Thin-edge bouldering provides the best medium to experiment and refine your technique, and to develop and maintain the necessary finger callouses.

"The importance of how you hold on to edges can not be overstated. When reaching for an edge, let your fingertips explore the edge's features and intricacies. Many holds, which at first feel marginal or even unusable, may feel considerably better with the slightest shifting of even one finger. So always shuffle your fingers over the whole edge. Make sure to get the thumb up to, or slightly over, the index finger. This substantially increases holding power and pulling force. Also, try to use only as much strength as is necessary to maintain your grip on the hold. Overcranking

(opposite)
Darrell Hensel on "Caliente," Suicide Rock, California.

Greg Epperson photo

wastes energy and inevitably puts more holes in fingertips that press down on razor-sharp edges. Hand and arm position also affect both the holding power and the way a hold feels; a slight change in their angle can make a hold feel much better, or worse.

"To stand on, and rely on – Nowhere does this axiom prove more important than on horrendous edging problems. Effective use of the feet must be mastered. And precision is of the utmost importance. There are three basic positions in which the foot may be placed to obtain maximum advantage from an edge. The most common of these is true side-edging, where the part of the shoe between the ball of the foot and the point of the boot (along the edge of the big toe) is placed precisely on the edge. Make sure the heel is up and out so maximum force can be directed down and in onto the edge. This is the most versatile form of edging, allowing the most mobility, both vertically and laterally. This type of edging also allows you to compensate for the use of other types of foot holds, and to maintain balance while putting together various sequences.

"Ball edging involves placing the edge of the boot at the ball of the foot precisely on the edge. This requires less toe strength and tends to be less strenuous on long, sustained edging problems. Its primary disadvantage is decreased sensitivity. It also puts your foot into a fixed position, providing very little mobility or chance for adjustment.

"Front pointing, which involves placing the point of the toe directly on the edge, proves most useful on bigger holds. This form of edging allows you to lean out more while you are climbing.

"The outside edge of the boot should not be forgotten as an option – though it can't be used on every route. The outside edge is particularly valuable when changing positions, say, from facing slightly left to facing slightly right. The ability to high step is no less valuable. A high step can allow you to use your feet even when the holds are few and far between. You can often avoid making a horrendous crank by stepping high enough to reach the next decent edge.

"Even if you plan carefully and use all of the mentioned techniques, you still occasionally will find yourself in that dreaded 'wrong foot' situation. When this happens, there are two possible solutions: Switch feet, or step through (jumping off isn't a viable option). When switching feet, you can support your weight by hanging on your fingers while moving one foot off the hold and placing the other onto it, or you can quickly shuffle one foot off, then the other foot on – sort of a controlled 'hop-step.' Either way, bear in mind that precision is the key here.

"If you choose to step through, you are again presented with a choice – stepping around in front, or behind, the set foot. No matter which way you step through – behind or in front – more caution is required than with the normal foot placement. You must pay careful attention to execution or you will force yourself out from and off the holds.

"When confronted with a baffling series of moves, you may find downclimbing (if possible) your most useful technique. This gives you the ability to re-evaluate your sequence and overall strategy.

"Some things to avoid while using your feet:
- Don't let your heel sag while standing on an edge;
- Don't overextend off your toe while reaching for the next hold;
- Try to keep your foot from moving on the edge.

"The abovementioned actions greatly decrease your boot's holding power and inevitably lead to losing that point of contact. Bunching the feet close together also should be avoided as it usually results in unstable or out-of-balance positioning.

"A casual attitude is usually a poor strategy to bring to a horrendous edging route. Upon arriving at the base of the route, scout for any obvious features or weaknesses. Try to piece these together into some type of overall plan. Then, when you start climbing, make each move with calculated precision, making sure the move flows logically into the next one. If possible, try to conceive entire sequences that will get you from one rest hold to the next. However, don't get so locked in to your approach or sequence that you can't improvise as needed. Two things are of primary importance: The ability to concentrate on what all four limbs are doing, and at the same time maintaining the right amount of force on each hold. Remember, above all, slab/edge climbing is an ongoing process of looking ahead, split second-decision making and precise technical execution."

Mari Gingery is one of the best and most experienced all-around climbers in the United States. Mari, along with Lynn Hill, first showed the rock climbing world that gender is no limitation. Those who feel otherwise are advised to watch her – and weep. Her vast experience runs from ghastly El Cap nail-ups to world-class free climbs. She is particularly magical on steep edging routes and the wisdom that follows helps to tell us why:

"First, note the temperature. Heat, humidity and direct sunlight can make a hard-edging climb horrendous. Wait for the shade and hope for a breeze to help keep your fingertips from pouring sweat. Your shoes should be relatively stiff with good (read 'not trashed') edges, but with enough flexibility to feel the rock through the soles. They should fit like a second skin, particularly forward of your arch. You don't want your foot rolling inside the shoe during a difficult edging move. Some climbers swear by plank-like boots, others by super-tight, lace-up slippers. I prefer a moderately-designed boot suitable for my specific weight. The heavier climber may desire a more substantial shoe. Regardless, the steeper the edging, the better a stiff boot works. Since difficult edging concentrates most of your weight on a very

Mari Gingery on the finals route, Snowbird, Utah

Beth Wald photo

small portion of your foot, a relatively comfortable fit is best. Lace snugly, but not painfully.

"Jitters and slapdash maneuvering lead to uncontrollable leg tremors and peelers. Before you start climbing, take a moment to calm your mind and focus your attention. A relaxed and confident attitude increases both your enjoyment and chances of success.

"Once collected and focused, scan the route for the line of least resistance to the first good stance. Mentally chart the best holds and plan a sequence that will most easily gain you a solid position. Hard-edging routes resemble climbing a convoluted ladder – with very small rungs, of course – but nevertheless a continuous series of steps. Consider your hands as points of balance and the means to direct body movement as you step from foothold to foothold. Only when the footholds become marginal do the hands increase their load bearing. The quickest way to burn out is to simply pull yourself from hold to hold, dragging your carcass behind. The notion is to expend the least amount of energy necessary to progress upwards. You'll have to divide your weight between your arms and legs, but always *keep as much weight as possible over your feet.*

"Precise foot placement is key on difficult edging because your point of contact is so minimal. Learn to place your boot accurately; if you need to shift your weight, do so until you can feel positive contact with the rock. Test what you can and cannot do on the boulders. Learn to trust your feet when you're on a sharp edge, and discover just how much weight you can place on a dime edge without popping off. Experiment to determine how you can achieve the most positive contact with the rock. Try standing on various points, from your big toe to the ball of your foot. Try the outside edge as well, the very toe, the heel – everywhere. Rotate your ankle to get the most boot rubber on the edge. Turning your foot sideways, parallel to the face, allows more of your edge to contact the rock, but also requires substantial hip 'turnout' to feel comfortable. Different climbers prefer different foot positions, so experiment to discover what works best for you.

"While clinging hard to handholds instills greater feelings of security, knowing where your feet are usually is more crucial. Also, to conserve hand strength (and fingertips), don't overgrip. Hold on just hard enough to stay put. 'Crimping' – lining up your fingertips on an edge and locking your thumb over your index finger – normally gives the best grip. But watch this technique – too much crimping can trash your fingers. To find the most positive grip, feel around the edge and adjust your fingers over the subtle irregularities – find the best placement before you pull on it. Sometimes even a minor adjustment can give a marginal hold a much surer feel.

"As you climb, carefully placing your feet on edges, concentrate on a smooth weight transfer from one foot to another. The legs supply the push; the hands direct your motion and give secondary support that is relative to how thin the footholds are. Maintain your balance with at least two – preferably three – points of support; two handholds and a foothold, or two footholds and a handhold. Move one limb at a time. As you move up, try to keep your center of gravity between your points of contact. For example, when traversing, you can counterbalance a leftward lean by extending your right leg out to the right. This also situates your weight and balance over your left foot – which is edging – and precludes the need to hang from an arm. For traversing sections, use cross-overs (one hand over or under the other) and step-throughs (inside or outside your supporting foot) to set up a reach to one side or the other. Shuffling hands and feet works, but often adds unnecessary moves. Hand and foot switches are tricky, but can be made more manageable by planning to leave space for the second hand or foot. A slick hand switch is to lift one or two fingers off a hold and replace them with fingers from the other hand. Foot switches can be executed as a well-timed hop and switch – which quickly can become an untimely hop and pop if poorly performed. When footholds are awkwardly spaced, consider taking several small steps to set up your foot position, rather than a single large step. Never rule out an extremely high step. Such a move can take the bite out of an otherwise thin crank by establishing a high foothold, which allows the leg, rather than the fingertips, to propel you up. Stout feet and calves help to maintain solid edging position without fatigue; strong thighs and gams help to leg out those high steps.

"Resting techniques, including very brief rest stops, are essential. You need time to look and think without exhausting your fingers. Good-sized edges provide obvious resting points. Stemming between footholds also lets you shake out and take a breather. Anytime you can get most of your weight over your feet for more than a few seconds, is time for rest. Taking brief breathers throughout a long section is a way to extend your stamina. After a high step, sitting on your heel is a stable, static, but temporary position from which you momentarily can get off your fingertips and scope the next moves. Use every chance to get off your arms and save your finger strength, as that will greatly extend the time you have to contemplate the next sequence. Pace yourself.

"Edging sequences often are devious and difficult to perceive quickly. To conserve strength, scan and evaluate upcoming moves from a rest point, then move quickly over the small footholds and thin pulls to the next relatively good stance. Linger briefly at relatively large holds to cool your fingertips and plot a course through the following section. Eye the route carefully, looking for obvious (and obscure) flakes and edges, points of protection and route meanderings. Visualize the sequence of moves that will lead to the next stance. If there is an obvious point on a route where a particular hand is required on a hold (i.e., where a route moves abruptly

Stepping through

sideways), think backwards down the handholds and determine which hand will start you off on the correct sequence. As you begin a difficult section, move quickly and smoothly. Keep looking around – especially down – for holds you may have overlooked. Keep a 'flow' of motion going until you reach the next stance. Don't think about any particular technique or tricks. Let your mind translate the pattern of holds into fluid motions. Experience will help you recognize shapes and patterns of holds and respond with appropriate moves. Strive for control. Be precise with your footwork. When you reach a point of uncertainty, it often is helpful to climb up a few moves and look around, get an idea of a probable sequence; then downclimb back to a stance to regroup before tackling the crux. Downclimbing from a puzzling section gives you time to feel out the holds, consider your sequence and recover somewhat before launching out again.

"Having linked handholds and footholds together into moves, and moves into sequences, you should think about clipping into some protection. Be sure your gear is organized and easily accessible before you leave the ground. Carry only what you will need, but be sure you have enough gear to gain the belay and clip yourself in. Many edging routes are bolt-protected and require only the use of carabiners. Normally, climbers clip into a bolt with a quickdraw; but a single locking carabiner also can be used to minimize a fall or ensure that the rope does not come unclipped. Good stances typically are found at each bolt, and these are secure places to rest and evaluate the remaining moves. Putting all of this information together with some imagination and desire should enable you to clip into the anchor bolts on your route.

"Thin-hold climbing is a tenuous type of ascent favoring balance, precision and control over raw strength. However, the honed footwork and balanced, controlled form acquired on difficult edging routes will help you climb steeper, more strenuous routes."

Common Mistakes in Slabbing and Edging:

- Not continuously scouring the face for best holds.
- Hugging, or laying against the rock (bad body position).
- Haphazard boot placement.
- Overloading boot with quick weight transfer, as opposed to smooth stepping onto footholds.
- Not keeping the boot still on the edge or allowing the boot to rotate on the edge once weighted.
- Overclinging with hands.
- Tensing up, climbing 'frozen.'
- Climbing 'heavy' as opposed to cat-like.
- Climbing too fast, or too slow – bad pacing.
- Abandoning form.
- Failure to judge the consequences of a fall.
- Climbing with the hands too low and the feet too high.
- Too little attention paid to predicting probable sequences.

Vertical
Adventures

Vertical face climbing is the rage. As touched upon in the introduction, modern climbers, in their search for more difficult routes, have turned *en masse* to the steep faces. In so doing, they have migrated from traditional areas like Yosemite Valley (where the glacier-polished granite does not afford sufficient holds), to countless new areas throughout the United States, from Smith Rock, Oregon, to Virginia's New River Gorge. Many of these new areas are long, low outcrops, or extended bluffs hedging rivers. The rock commonly is sandstone, limestone or a funky conglomerate, very steep and amply fitted with holds and pockets – perfect for vertical adventures. These steep crags often lack the easy ability to accept natural protection, however, so bolts are the dominant anchor. No longer shackled by the values and ethics of the established cliffs, climbers at these new areas have adopted a new means of protecting the leader – in a word, pre-placing protection – thus making otherwise impossible walls assailable. Whether you or I have a beef with these methods is beside the point. There's no holding back the limit, and pre-placing protection was inevitable. Once the angle kicks up to vertical, we're looking at a whole new ball game. The falls are more abrupt and stressful, the protection is further taxed and the sheer effort involved in climbing these routes usually is much more.

SOME KIND OF POWERFUL

As a rule, the steeper the route, the more strenuous it will be. Even on moderate routes following jug-holds from bottom to top, you still have to use your arms, which tire in a hurry regardless of your fitness. Overall strength, then, plays a key role in all steep face climbing. Those who have it and know how to use and conserve it tend to be your ace steep-face climbers.

Power Rationing

In dealing with slabs and edging routes, we talked about pacing, rhythm and the necessity of climbing using the least effort. The need to husband your strength is even more important with vertical face climbing, principally because you rarely can get the kind of rest that allows you to recapture spent gas. The steeper the climbing becomes, the more vital it is to conserve strength so it's there when you most need it.

(opposite)
Dale Goddard on "Scar Face," Smith Rock, Oregon.

Greg Epperson photo

PRINCIPLES

It's a maxim for all forms of climbing that you keep your weight over your feet. It's necessary in friction climbing because often there are no handholds. To a great degree, the same goes with edging. With steep face climbing, your arms will flame out unless your feet continually support your weight. The tendency is to yard primarily with the arms – and that is dead wrong. Never underestimate the value of any foothold, however skimpy. Even the slightest purchase with your feet makes a considerable difference. For example, if you can unweight yourself just slightly on a pull-up bar – perhaps by having a buddy tug on your belt loop – you can chin yourself another dozen times.

All the footwork tricks we covered in the previous chapters hold true with vertical face climbing as well. But now, everything's more strenuous, calf (edging) strength is all the more essential, and body position is different.

Suck It In

Once the angle of the rock reaches vertical, your torso will actually overhang your feet unless it is pasted against the stone. The more your torso is angled back beyond a vertical posture over your feet – the more you lean out – the harder it is to hang on. When you suck your body into the wall, you are shifting weight off your arms and onto your boots. It's a good practice, but does not always mean the climb will be less strenuous on your arms.

We've already called the relaxed X body position the most natural and least strenuous. Same goes here. If your arms are somewhat extended to decent holds, sucking your torso into the wall does ease the strain because your weight is better situated over your shoes. But if the hands are positioned below the shoulders – even if they are latched onto good holds – it becomes very strenuous. Remember, the sharper the angle formed by your lower and upper arm, the more strenuous the position is. Conversely, the more straight your arms are, the more bone structure (instead of contracted muscles) can bear the load, resulting in a less strenuous posture. Of course, as you move upward and past holds, your arms become increasingly contracted. Avoid stopping in a compressed attitude. You don't want to hang out very long with your arms bent and your muscles contracting. Keep reaching above – to a side-pull, to any hold that will allow you to get your arms straight. Try and maintain long lines of limb, letting bone structure absorb the tension. Stay balled up too long and you'll be yelling, 'Watch me!'

As I delve deeper into things, breaking moves down

> **To drive it home:**
>
> - Draw your body to the rock when the holds allow and the position feels natural.
> - Keep your arms straight whenever possible – particularly when surveying the rock above – letting bones, not contracted muscles, bear the load.
> - Once you have pulled yourself into a contracted position, arms bent and cranking, toes edging madly on holds, try to quickly extend into the relaxed X position.

further and further, I'm bound to sound pedantic about what are otherwise natural movements. I risk that in an attempt to boil things down to the basic elements – to discover what can go wrong and what is optimal. Again, conscious recognition of body position and moves is the best method to correctly program your neuro-muscular processes.

STATIC CLIMBING: VICIOUS CRANK

Vicious cranks usually are required to span long sections of rock between usable holds. This process involves several sequential phases. The whole process can be broken down like this: Crank, step, lockoff, reach, extend (explained in detail below). You extend back into the relaxed X position – or an approximation of it – to get 'set-up' to repeat the process. Each phase blends into the other, sometimes overlapping; but by breaking down the individual movements, we can better understand the unavoidable 'centipede progression,' as well as examine what can go right, or wrong, and and begin making the knowledge an instinct.

Let's jump right into the middle of a hard crux section and look at the succession of different movements. Phase one is the . . .

(1) Set-Up Phase

Your body is static, at least momentarily. You're standing on holds, legs somewhat extended, hands over your head or extended to the side. The boots bear maximum weight as you jockey your fingers around on the holds, getting set up. However precarious the posture, you must try to relax here, to save strength and inhibit any wobbling on the holds. Acknowledge that whenever you've stopped, such as during this set-up phase, your toes will start to fatigue at a rate relative to how poor a hold you're standing on. If the holds are minimal, it's essential to keep the edge firm and not hop around on the edge. Unless the foothold is a big one, move on before your tired calf forces movement on the hold. In extreme cases, when your feet are splayed onto weird slopers in imbalanced attitudes, each second's pause makes popping off more probable. It then becomes a feat of concentration to stay tight on the holds, however poor they may be. Also, it is during this set-up phase that you most easily can suck your hips and torso in close to the rock. This puts even more pressure on the feet; but they are better prepared to take the load than the arms. If you can shake out an arm here, do it, but quickly. (Up to 90 percent

of your strength can be recovered in 45 seconds, but it takes many minutes, sometimes hours, to get back to 100 percent.

And if you're really pumped, you'll have to wait a couple days to get it all back.)

Okay. Your lower body is perched on desperate turf to allow your hands the chance to get 'set up' for the ensuing crank. Simultaneously, your eyes are scanning the rock, reckoning the various sequence options overhead. Obviously, I can hardly second-guess the subsequent moves, but there are several things that can make your present, probably desperate posture at least manageable.

As you set one hand, usually reaching the free hand high, the tendency is to overcling with the clasping hand. Be aware of this. If chalking up will increase your chances of pinging off, skip the chalk for that move. And watch your breathing. Don't hold your breath – that will only tense you up. Once your grip is set on the best available holds, you must quickly determine what holds you are pulling up to, and what footholds you will use. Do not simply start cranking, hoping you can reckon the next move once you're a little higher. The Set-Up Phase is far and away the best time to try to reckon and visualize the following moves; so always strive to have a probable sequence in your head before pulling into the . . .

(2) Crank/Step Phase

Because we're all quadrupeds, the crank/step phase is unavoidable, and means most every sequence will require it in one form or another.

Starting this phase, the arms are extended and the hands are clasping edges. The next move is to place one or the

other foot up to a higher edge, simultaneously crank with the arms, and step onto the edge. In so doing, we naturally move from the relaxed X position of the set-up phase into the collapsed X position. This phase, when executed, is what we refer to as 'doing the move,' though the start and finish to such a move or sequence is rarely so well-defined. The trick is to make sure one move is followed by another move.

First, the climb dictates what hold we're going to step on to. Make certain the boot is set ideally. Falls are most common in this phase, and usually result when the hastily-placed boot blows off the edge as we start weighting it. Hands blowing off holds is rarer, but still common. On truly bleak cruxes, climbers often fall mid-way through this crank/step phase. Either the foot has blown off, or they've bungled their positioning during the set-up phase, or the power just wasn't there to execute the crank.

When you start the actual crank, you want deliberate movement, not jerky, power-loading of either hand or footholds, which probably are marginal anyway. Even when you are climbing semi-dynamically, you still want a fluid pull with the arms and a gingerly weighting of the foothold. Often, the hardest part of the crank simply is getting started, because it requires initiating a burst of power to the holds. Try to be fluid, rather than jerky or sudden, when you need to pour on the power. Once the arms are even slightly bent, it usually becomes much easier to crank. When starting the crank simply is impossible without a boost of some kind, consider a quick, Elvis-esque hip thrust, which will push your torso closer to the wall and help get the crank started.

As you initiate the crank and step onto the higher foothold, the free foot ideally should move onto another edge as well. If that is unlikely, and the step is a high one, a little light paddling with the free foot can provide valuable upward body English. There is a subtle but very fundamental element of timing involved here, particularly if the move is so hard as to require explosive strength. This power timing – coordinating the limbs and hips in a quick, fluid, upward burst – is best understood and mastered on the boulders.

Once you have cranked up, you have to pause at the . . .

(3) Lockoff

This is not really a phase, but is worth studying because so many falls occur at this point. You're cranked up, probably on poor holds. Your leg is bent, boot edging madly on a hold – another bad one, most likely. You want to press out the foothold a bit more, get that leg straight or nearly straight, and get your weight on it.

But before this is possible, you must get your hands well established on higher holds. You've pulled up on the present handholds, and soon will have to hang on one hold – locking your body off on it – while the free hand reaches for another, higher hold. The key here is the lockoff on the clinging hand.

Rarely will handholds all be horizontal ones. Often, you're cranking on various side-pulls, pinches, etc. Regardless, the most secure position – the one that best maintains the locked-off position - is when your elbow is drawn into your side – 'elbow to lat,' in parlance. Note that when you've chinned yourself up on a bar, then try to let go with one hand, still keeping your chin to the bar, you can do so only when your elbow is tucked to your lat (lat = latissimus dorsi muscle). Move your elbow out even slightly and you'll thaw right off the bar. So when you have to let go with one hand and reach for a higher hold, always try to juke your torso toward the locked-off hand, getting the elbow to your side. This works well even with side-pulls. Also, if you can splay your legs and draw your pelvis closer to the rock, it becomes less strenuous. This is not always possible, of course, particularly when balance is so critical that you can't juke your body without pitching off. A climber who has reached this impasse most often will slap for a higher hold, trying to snatch it before the clinging hand fades. Also, sometimes you will not be able to crank up high enough to get the elbow to the lat. In this case, try to get your near shoulder as close to the clasping hand as possible. This technique requires more strength, but is far more secure.

When the holds are too small or the position too tenuous to allow a lockoff, you are left to execute a 'dead point,' which will be explained later.

(4) Extension/Installation Phase

The installation phase takes you from the compressed and locked-off phase, to a phase where your posture is in some form of the relaxed X. In short, after you have locked off, then reached for higher holds, you must extend far enough to 'install' yourself back into the 'set-up' position. (Note how virtually all moves go through this centipede-like progression – crank, step, lockoff, reach, extend, then 'setting-up' to repeat the process.)

Since your hands already are low, and you can't change the hold beneath your driving leg, you've got to install your hands on higher holds so you can press the leg out. If you're fortunate, you'll have two footholds, but it's uncanny how often you'll find that during the crank/step phase, you're pressing out a single foothold. Anyway, balance *and* strength are key here.

As you jockey your hands onto higher holds – as you pull and extend into the set-up posture (relaxed X) – the weight-bearing foot must remain exactly placed. If you've stayed on it through the crank/step phase, it probably won't blow if you can remain tight. The trick is to distribute your weight on a second foothold as soon as you are able.

Remember that you rarely can get a rest anywhere save in the set-up phase. Perhaps you can stop briefly in lockoff phase, if your foot is on a suitable hold, but maintaining this posture for long is usually more strenuous than moving on. So as a general rule, we can say the faster you get installed into the set-up posture, back into the relaxed X position, the more energy you will save.

Breaking things down into phases has simplified – or perhaps oversimplified – vertical face climbing. Climbing sequences vary so much that it's difficult to to discuss in any but the most generic terms. Still, we've discovered some truths, also generic, which will apply more often than not. Now it is time to look at those times when they will not.

(1) Set-Up Phase Objectives:
- Assume relaxed X position, or closest posture to it;
- Get hands extended onto best holds for the crank to follow;
- Reckon probable crank sequence;
- Chalk if possible;
- Suck torso into rock, over feet, if possible.

Set-Up Phase Mistakes:
- Moving the boot, which pops off hold;
- Overclinging with hands;
- Pausing too long to chalk, if the holds don't allow;
- Choosing the wrong handholds for the following move;
- Not reckoning the next moves;
- Holding your breath and tensing up;
- Standing on one edge when another is available for free foot.

(2) Crank/Step Phase Objectives:
- Controlled upward movement;
- Selecting best foothold, placing boot precisely thereon and fluidly loading 'stepping' foot, getting it to bear optimum weight;
- Remaining balanced despite the strain;
- Maintaining smooth power throughout the 'crank.'

Crank/Step Phase Mistakes:
- Imprecise placement of 'stepping' foot or excessive, jerky loading of foot which results in blowing off the hold;
- Getting stuck at mid-crank;
- Choosing the wrong hand holds, which results in an un-doable sequence.

(3) Lockoff Phase Objectives:
- Momentarily remain secure before reaching for higher handholds;
- Quickly survey and visually verify next move, or quickly revise 'probable sequence;'
- Set free foot on edge (if possible) to better distribute weight; maintain secure lockoff, keeping elbow to lat whenever possible.

Lockoff Phase Mistakes:
- Not cranking high enough;
- Not getting elbow to lat when possible;
- Not getting hips close to the rock;
- Letting the foot move on the edge and rotate off;
- Incorrectly reckoning next hand holds.

(4) Installation Phase Objectives:
- Getting 'installed' on next hand holds (grabbing correct edge) and straightening out 'pushing' leg;
- Extending into relaxed X posture;
- Getting both feet on best available holds.

Installation Phase Mistakes:
- Clinging hand melts off as free hand reaches;
- Free hand reaches for the wrong hold, loads it immediately, and you fall;
- Foot blows off hold as you fully extend leg;
- Free foot doesn't seek out edge.

STEMMING

Stemming, or "bridging", is the process of counter-pressuring with the feet off slanting holds. The classic stem  problem occurs in right-angled corners, where the crack is so poor that the climber must ratchet his limbs up via counter-pressure. Often, the applied pressure is improbable and very marginal, particularly on steep face routes, where the holds are normally poor or sloping. And it's not just a task for the feet. Often the hands must counter-pressure against the holds. Essentially, your body is like a spring loaded between two apposing holds. The only thing holding the spring in place is their purchase at both ends, and the tension between them. Moving the spring up, then, is the tricky bit, as the tension must go lax for a second. Yet it never can. Often it is the diagonal pressure of one hand against one foot that keeps you on the wall, and the climber alternates this bridge in moving up. The variations are endless: you may back-step with one boot, smear with the other, palm with one hand, and crimp a dime with the other. Flexibility and balance are key. And supple ankles are a must. Many times the stem is less valuable in gaining height as it is in gaining a quasi rest. If you can manage a solid stem on a steep route, it gives you a good foundation to shake each arm out in turn, snatch a breath, and survey what's ahead. The art of stemming is a tricky one, and the practice becomes less and less likely as the angle steepens.

DYNAMIC CLIMBING

Dy-nam-ic: also known as a 'lunge,' a 'dynamo,' a 'mo,' all requiring the climber to propel himself toward a distant hold in the hopes of grabbing it.

The previous look at phases assumed that the climbing was controlled and static. However, as the angle steepens and the holds run thinner and farther apart, dynamic climbing increasingly comes into play. Many times, gently bounding over the difficulties is far less strenuous than slow, static movement. Let's look at the standard techniques.

Powerglide

Say you're in the set-up phase, in the relaxed X posture – legs extended, boots on holds, hands extended and clasping. The problem? The next handhold is way the hell up there. The handholds between your present position and the next are too scant to pull up and lockoff; perhaps even if you did crank, step and lockoff, your reach still would be shy of that next handhold. You might be able to span this stretch with a Herculean static move, but that would leave you so torched you couldn't carry on. You're looking, then, at a classic chance to 'powerglide.'

The powerglide

The powerglide is a controlled dynamic. You begin just as you would if you were initiating the crank/step phase. Once your hands are set, you toe a higher edge. If the foothold is in line with your body, it's straightforward to get some thrust off of it. If you have to stem a foot out to the side, the physics are all wrong for upward drive, and the foothold is of negligible value. You do not simply throw yourself upward off marginal handholds with no consideration to the foothold. If anything, the foothold is more crucial than the handholds. Anyway, once the foot is placed on the higher edge, you must generate sufficient thrust – by yanking with the hands, keeping the hips in and quickly extending off the foothold – that your vector will carry you past the lockoff point and to within slapping range of the higher hand hold. In other words, you 'powerglide' to that next hold.

Make certain the boot is placed precisely on the edge. Ninety percent of the time the extending leg provides the upwards thrust; the hands only initiate the glide (also, keep your torso close to the rock). When your leg extends, the boot's edge must maintain accelerating mass well beyond your actual weight. The edge will blow off unless it is precisely placed, and the attitude and positioning of the toes must remain constant. Remember, maintaining contact with the rock means maintaining control. In maximum powergliding, you might actually have to toe high off the hold, stretching your heel way up for that added inch – but your boot must never become dislodged from the hold. You never actually jump off the edge unless you're going a mighty long ways, and the sought-after handhold is sufficient to support all of your body weight on its own. In other words, leaving the rock completely in a desperate reach for a handhold is virtually impossible to execute successfully unless you're gliding for a plentiful hold – like a jug. Gliding around off little tweakers is reserved for Captain Granitic. Let's go through the motions.

You're set up, hands and feet on holds, poised. You spot the high handhold, a ways above, and decide to powerglide to it. You surgically place your boot on a higher hold, which must be good enough to bear the thrusting leg. (Better an edge – even a small one – than a smear.) Then, you lock your eyes back onto that higher hold as a Zen archer would draw a bead on his target – a solitary grain of brown rice. In one coordinated burst, keeping your hips in, you heave with the hands; and as your weight comes onto the foothold, you quickly but fluidly extend your leg, pushing your body into dynamic motion, powergliding up. As you glide past where you'd normally lockoff, your hand keeps clasping hard, pulling strong.

Slap it! How soon you release a free hand to slap for the higher hand hold depends how good, or poor, the clasped holds are. There are many degrees of powergliding. Skilled climbers often powerglide all over a pitch, avoiding more strenuous static moves. In a situation where all holds are ample – the thrusting foothold, the pulling handhold, and the hold the climber's gliding for – he can avoid a grievous lockoff and simply powerglide to the next hold, nice and easy-like, executing more of a quick reach and latch than an all-out slap. If the handholds are bleak, however, a climber should wait till he's reached the top of his glide, then quickly slap for the hold. Like a fly ball, the climber is momentarily weightless at the apex of the glide – the dead point – and that's when you release a hand and slap for the next hold.

Latch it! Remember three things about this stage of the dynamo. First, the slapped hand must hit the hold exactly; it must be a bull-eye. Secondly, the fingers most often should land in the cling-grip configuration. Trying to latch a hold with a claw grip is risky at best – the fingers can just curl off if you must immediately power-load the hold. Thirdly, try to generate enough height with the glide that you're not latching with a fully extended arm. If the arm is slightly bent, the muscles are set to exert the necessary clinging power. Overshooting is possible, but more likely on all-out dynamos.

The powerglide is a standard face-climbing technique, requiring precise timing, coordination, considerable contact and explosive strength, and a certain natural athleticism. The technique most readily is mastered on boulders. Learning the intricacies of dynamic climbing on the lead is like learning to drive by racing the Indianapolis 500 – not a sound plan.

A lesser, more delicate form of the power glide – the 'dead point' – will be taken up later. For now, understand that this 'dead point' refers to that split second when the climber is weightless, at the apex of a lunge, when he is neither going up nor down. Though describing this moment of weightlessness, dead point also refers to a form of dynamic move. Rather than propelling your body upwards, the dead point usually involves dynamically drawing your body into the rock – usually vertical or overhanging rock – and at the 'dead point,' flashing a hand up for a higher hold. In the following chapters we will hear plenty more about this important technique.

Side-glide

Occasionally, it is necessary to chuck a lateral dynamic. The process does not significantly differ from vertical power gliding. If you're required to cover a pretty good stretch, it's almost always a matter of dynamically rocking over onto a foothold and either semi-falling, or flinging yourself sideways. Whether falling or flinging, you're not going to be successful without a workable foothold. Oftentimes, said hold will slope in the direction of thrust. Success depends on the aforementioned factors; but it is even more crucial with side-gliding that the prospective handhold be a good one, preferably slanting your way. If you're thinking of side-gliding way to the flanks, hoping to stick a poor hold that slopes away from you, you'd better have a hardy belay and a bolt at your waist.

So far, I've talked about body position and power and offered some hints on conserving it, as well as discussed the different phases of movement, and touched briefly on dynamic climbing. We can pick things apart only so far without ending up with a bag of abstractions. Time to look at the large picture.

FLASH IT!

Says 'Cocoa' Joe Sloan: "The best way to climb anything is to walk up to it, draw a breath, and solo the bastard." Coarsely put, but there's no arguing Joe's point. If everyone knew they would never fall, no one would ever use a rope. The next best thing to soloing is a 'flash' ascent – climbing the route, no falls, on your first try – which amounts to essentially the same thing as Joe's method. You've simply used gear – just in case you fall.

The previous sections on strategy and modus operandi (covered in slab and edging chapters) apply here as well. Those sections all were geared to help a climber scale a route on his first try. To do so, he should study the topo, quiz other climbers about particulars, scope the route from below and incorporate the recommendations on the physical aspects of climbing.

Though not qualitatively different than lower-angled routes, vertical adventures require more from the climber, so let's look at some special considerations:

Already mentioned were matters of Focus, Form and Rythm, the need to maintain concentration of the job at hand, to never forget your finest technique, and to keep a pace that balances constant upward progress with resting. If anything, more of all three are needed once the angle hits vertical – particularly pacing. Regardless of a climb's numerical rating, most every steep face route involves stringing moves together between 'good' holds. 'Good' may mean only a transitory hold, where you can briefly pause, or a hold not part of a crux sequence. Such a hold is likely to be at the start or the end of a grim stretch. In a simplified sense, 'good' holds will, or should, dictate your pace – how fast you climb between the good holds, and, once gained, how long you stay at them. Before saying more, understand that it's almost always better to try and de-pump by standing on these "good" holds, rather than by hanging off them and trying to shake out one arm at a time. Regardless, you should always scout the pitch from below, and know where any good holds are, or appear to be. This helps you formulate a probable strategy. Remember, however, that more than one plan has been abandoned upon discovering that what looked 'bomber' from below turned out to be a glazed bowling ball once clasped.

My strategy here is again to break the route into various sections – this time between 'good' holds. A common mistake is to devise a strategy based on where the bolts or protection are. Particularly on modern, 'clip-and-go' routes, the bolts have been installed on a toprope, thus a bolt by no means signals a break in the action. Also, you never know who placed the bolts – it could have been an utter pinhead with no concept of position, or it could have been someone who thoughtfully installed the bolts to facilitate easy, or at least possible, clips. Since virtually all clip-and-go routes are at least adequately protected, injury rarely is the problem. Climbing them is. That's why, generally, climbers map out a strategy according to where the good holds are, and consider a grim clip part of the overall sequence.

The idea is simple: Reduce the route to sections between good holds, then start estimating where the most strenuous bits will be. That done, factor in the location of the crux. Now, you can estimate what parts will require the most effort, where you should try and cop a decent rest, and how fast or slow you should move over given sections. Once you have the route cased, you are free, and advised, to deal with one section at a time. This sectionalizing gives you an idea of what to expect, and can positively effect your overall success. It does not, however, help you overcome individual moves. The previous talk of phases, etc., was geared to help you execute sequences.

There are two aspects to climbing hard sections – predicting the best sequence, then doing it. Face climbs often are spangled with chalk marks. These help to identify holds, but also mislead because they don't tell you which holds are useful, and which are useless. Remember, chalk marks tell a story, but the tale is a confusing one. The real value of chalk marks is in delineating a hold that you might not have seen otherwise. Whether that hold is of any value is your call.

Watching your partner (or anyone) do a sequence is instructional, but you can run into problems when trying to duplicate another climber's moves down to the smallest nuance. A person's strengths, technique, dimensions and flexibility can mean that what was easy for he, might be impossible for thee. Everyone must discover their own best way.

An example: For several years, I did most of my free climbing with Lynn Hill, who certainly is one of the world's great climbers. She could splay her legs out like Olga Korbut, do magical things while being absolutely balled up, had the kind of balance and staying power I could only dream about, and seemed fearless of any potential fall. I had a little more experience, a tad more explosive strength, a 12-inch reach advantage and about 100 additional pounds to haul around. We could rarely do things as the other had, and attempts to do so were frustrating for each of us. Often, we climbed the same route in completely different manners. Only a few times could she not climb something I could, and then only because the one and only hold simply was beyond her reach. Otherwise, she floated up everything I did, often in the lead, and often with far greater ease than I had.

The same thinking applies to 'betas,' which are blow-by-blow breakdowns of a given route. Casual betas are simply what one climber tells another, the narrative usually accompanied by lavish body contortions that physically describe the climbing. Formal betas can be fabulous for their detail, and sometimes are drafted on graph paper with an attending written drift of the rarest crag lingo. The generic information is almost always useful, but beyond that, be careful when trying to execute the beta to the letter. You're glad to know that you should layback here, or reach for the hidden bucket there; but as far as 'crimping, then matching on the flange and hucking for the burnished wart' – well, I wouldn't be slave to such advice. Caress the flange and eyeball the wart, certainly, but don't force yourself into a sequence that doesn't feel right.

In summary, let's listen to Christian Griffith, who's forged himself an international reputation for scaling some the hardest steep face climbs from France to Flagstaff. Says Christian:

"Some of the world's most classic and historical routes are vertical face climbs. On no other angle does the coordination of a climber's limbs, as well as the integration of different kinds of movement, play such a significant role in ascent. Also, vertical face climbs serve as the best training ground for the latest vogue of overhanging test pieces.

"An even distribution of weight on both hands and legs is essential. Precision on reaches often is measured in millimeters. Body tension and the conservation of energy are paramount for success. Only on vertical rock can all of these elements be learned.

"When on particularly scant holds, think of each individual move as having two parts – anticipation and execution. Every move, big or small, alters your balance point. You must anticipate this, and adjust by shifting your weight. This is best accomplished with hip movement, sometimes exaggerated. Whatever the extent of hip movement, the point is to climb deliberately. Anticipating and adjusting before a move helps eliminate any swaying or jiggling once you start cranking.

" 'Turn out' is a tricky concept, and refers to the hip's proximity to the rock in relation to the relative height of the feet. Perfect turn out would find a climber's butt as low as his heels, while having the knees splayed out and hips pressed against the wall. Turn out facilitates lateral and vertical mobility, while allowing the feet to absorb maximum weight. Getting used to the concept of turn out – which essentially refers to the ability to open up your hips – best can be learned on the slabs. Again, the idea is to keep your butt as close to your heels as possible, while keeping your hips close to the rock. You will not always want to climb in this squat posture, but it is an invaluable technique when the need arises.

"A crucial technique is the 'dead point.' I refer here to a short form of dynamic that permits long reaches when a lack of power or an awkward stance make a static reach impossible. An all-out dynamic will sometimes span four feet of rock; a powerglide is a lesser form of the all-out dyno; a dead point, however, rarely exceeds an arm's length in distance. While the all out dynamic primarily is a matter of generating and controlling upward locomotion; a dead point emphasizes the body's inward movement. In short, we can dynamically suck our body toward the rock, and at the moment when we're weightless – the dead point – we can flash a hand up to the desired hold. Remember, the closer you are to the rock, the more extension you have off your feet and the higher your reach.

"Dead points often are performed off the most minuscule holds. The execution must be precise, and for the split second at the dead point, when your torso has been drawn to the rock and your hand flashes up for the next hold, your body must remain absolutely still. Once you clasp the hold, you'll make small and instantaneous adjustments that allow you to hang on. Again, try to anticipate the play of your balance point so that when you do reach, your position is the most comfortable one that can be held unwaveringly until latching that next hold. Accuracy and timing are key. Remember not to direct your dynamic energy exclusively upward, as you would in an all-out dynamo, but diagonally up and in. A quick, strong pop with the hips is the best way to initiate this motion, particularly if the handholds are small.

"It is common for climbers to think of their hands only as a set of fingers, and to consider only the front soles of their boots. Correct modes of conserving strength and enhancing power requires some rethinking of these concepts. By using my thumbs, I can greatly increase my holding power. Sometimes, rather than wrapping my thumb over my index finger, as in a crimp, I will place my thumb directly on a hold, then wrap my fingers over the thumb. This will limit your range of motion in certain instances, but when the situation is right – with both straight pulls and hangs – this thumb technique can boost my power some 50 percent.

"On bigger holds, notably knobs and horns, I often wrap the heel of my hand over them. This sometimes gives me a much better grip than I would get by clasping the same hold with my fingers. A limited technique, yes, but I have found it a very effective way to rest my forearms, particularly during competition climbing.

"You'll often see people using their feet as stumps, as though they've lost all sensation from the big toe back. Granted, the bulk of your footwork takes place between the arch and the big toe, but the rear part of the foot also has utility. On several desperate routes, I found that by high-stepping directly onto my heel I attained faster and better balance than had I stood on the ball of my foot. This heel technique is rarely used, but is a good trick for getting a quick reach, or grabbing a moment's rest.

"I've also found that using slippers has greatly increased my foot awareness. Slippers allow you to use your feet like your hands, as their supple form curls over the edges and actually pulls you into the rock.

"Climbing is no dance. You need ballet-like precision in the midst of extreme physical effort, but there is nothing artfully contrived in vertical face climbing. Success hangs on efficiency and conserving energy. Styles amongst top climbers vary from fluid to mechanical, but the goal always is to move one part of the body while making minimum demands on the rest. Maintaining a balance of energy on the limbs is crucial, and disrupting this equilibrium – often measured in ounces – can fumble a dead point or send your foot off a key hold. Kinesthetic sense results in consistency, consistency in success."

Colin Lantz on "Chains of Love,"
Flatirons, Colorado.

Beth Wald photo

Overhanging Face

By now you should well understand the basic tenets of face climbing: Maintaining shrewd body position, a relaxed bearing and precise placement of hands and feet while conserving energy and climbing aggressively over crux sections – plus the need to always look, and plan, ahead. These notions all directly apply to overhanging face climbing. However, as the rock steepens, gravity changes the physics involved, and body position must take account, and adjust to, factors unique to overhanging rock. The technique of pulling up on holds, as well as the consequent arm and lower torso position, varies from that used on vertical terrain. Because overhanging routes usually are more strenuous than vertical climbs of even the same rating, technical adjustments generally are aimed at conserving limited strength.

HINGE IT

Check out any playground where kids swing on the jungle gym. Note how they can stay on the bars for a very long time. Note also that their arms are like broom straws, and you'll realize that it's not just muscular strength that's keeping them up there. Finally, note that they always hang and swing from straight arms. They simply don't have the power to start locking the bar off – never mind chinning themselves on it. These kids use two vital skills that apply to climbing overhanging rock: Try and always keep your arms straight, and consider your shoulders a hinge.

As mentioned a dozen times, you should keep your arms straight whenever possible, for it allows the bones, rather than constricted muscles, to bear much of the weight. But even arrow-straight limbs cannot keep your forearms from burning when they are working overtime to keep the fingers clasping the holds. With proper conditioning, the forearms can manage the stress. The back muscles, though, require enormous energy – of which even the best climber has a limited amount – to pull up and lockoff a hold on overhanging terrain. Because most overhanging routes require you to pull up and lockoff somewhere – if not many times – you'll want to conserve the

Straight arm hang is the most effective rest.

John Sherman photo

back muscles by trying to climb with straight arms whenever possible. That way, when the lockoff comes, you'll have the gas to perform it. Learning to use your shoulders as a hinge, while letting your driving legs provide the upward thrust, is the trick to keeping the arms straight while continuing upward movement.

Both the concept and the mechanics are basic. Your hands clasp holds, and straight arms lead back to your shoulders. As the legs fluidly push off foot holds, the torso levers up with the shoulders as the hinge point. If you visualize this, you'll see that the farther you push/hinge your torso out with your feet, the farther your head moves out from under your hands. On extremely overhanging routes, like roofs, it feels somewhat natural to have your head directly below your hands, in line with straight arms, as gravity dictates. When you thrust out with your legs, however, you're pushing your head past the natural gravity point. While this saves the back muscles, it stresses the forearms in proportion to how far your head goes past the gravity point, or how far you hinge out. Ideally, you'll want to reach for a higher hold close to the time when your torso reaches the gravity point. When you pass that point, you'll either have to suck in and lockoff, then reach, or perform a quasi-dynamic little hinge swing to reach that upper hold.

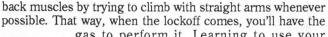

The body hangs off a straight arm to allow the shoulder to act as a hinge for the reach above.

John Sherman photo

FEET

Your feet perform two essential functions on overhanging rock: supporting your lower torso, and providing push for upward movement. Realize that if your feet are not placed properly or hooked on something, you'll be left hanging entirely from your arms – the worst position on an overhanging route because your arms will burn out in a matter of yards, and that will be that. Most of the time, you should strive to look for and utilize a combination of both hooks and pushing footholds. First, let's talk about the hooks.

No one climbs a blank, overhanging wall. The more the route overhangs, the more (and better) holds there tend to be. That means there will be places for your feet, though you'll have to work at finding the most secure spots. Let's start with the really overhanging stuff – routes steeper than 120 degrees.

Because much of your body is back and under your hands, gravity wants to peel your feet off any hold and leave you hanging straight up and down, directly under your beleaguered arms. Consequently, there always is a constant pull on your feet – as though weights were attached to your heels. Simply placing your foot on a good edge does not always work well. On routes that are just over vertical, this is

John Sherman photo

not so much a problem. But once the angle really starts to kick back, you must try to get your foot lodged, or hooked, on or between holds.

The easiest way to understand the problem is to picture yourself jamming out a roof crack. Said crack provides solid jams for both your hands and your feet, the appendages twisted in the crack. But say that you can't get your feet into the crack. Even if the underside of the roof has 1-inch edges, simply toeing them while upside down won't work. The only way to keep your feet on those edges would involve using titanium abdominal muscles to keep your legs supported and straight. You'd be climbing in a sort of front lever position, which is more strenuous than just dangling off the jams. Anyway, since none of us have titanium abs, you can see the need to get some kind of hook for your feet to support your lower torso.

John Sherman photo

Captain Hook

The standard hook is the heel variety. The exact positioning depends entirely on the available hold. On a bucket edge, say, one commonly uses the very end of the heel. On smaller holds, you will have to jockey the heel around and use whatever part bites best. Whatever the position, you'll want to both drape the heel on the hold and apply a little downward pressure to keep the heel well-seated. The more your leg is bent, the more pressure you'll want to apply. Once the leg is extended, sufficient downward pressure occurs naturally as gravity attempts to rip your heel off the hold. Remember that the rand, the heel cup, or any of the ancillary rubber on the upper part of the boot is usually of the same 'sticky' stuff that the sole is made of. Try to get some of this tacky matter on the hook, whatever the foot's position on the hold.

Marginal Hook

Insecure heel and foot hooks call for ingenuity on the part of the climber. Lodge it, jam it, hook it on the rand, or even on the shoe laces, pry it with the toes, but by all means, get that foot hooked on something. Sometimes a good hold is facing the wrong way, away from you. If you can get one foot in a position to push, you often can snag the other toe on the away-facing hold, and pull with it. The opposing pressure between the two feet will help keep your torso locked in.

Heel hook above the center of gravity to reduce the weight on the arms.

John Sherman photo

Straight arms and
opposition techniques to
keep the feet on – the left
pushes, the right pulls.

John Sherman photo

LEGENDARY ABS

Legendary abdominals are but one step beneath titanium abs. And believe it – you'll greatly benefit from a set on overhanging terrain. Since your torso hinges at the waist and is never connected to the rock – save when hang-dogging – the abs are the bridge between your points of contact – i.e. your hands and feet. They keep your torso straight when required, and are remarkably taxed when doing so. There is no mystery to getting legendary abs – all it takes is hard work. (Remember that incline sit-ups tend to work only the upper ab. Leg and knee raises hit the lower abs, which take much of the stress in truly overhanging climbing.)

There are many possible sequence progressions that require the use of legendary abs. One of the most common – and strenuous – involves using both hooks and thrusting holds for the feet. Say your hands are set and you're eyeballing the next set of holds. One foot is hooked, the other ready to thrust off a hold. As you thrust with the leg and pull/hinge with the arms and shoulders, often you'll have to free the hooked foot to get enough height to reach the next handhold. That means you must simultaneously release the hook and thrust off the foot, hinging off the shoulder. Then, you must let go with one hand and reach above. For a moment, you're hanging on only one arm, with your thrusting foot pasted on a hold and without that stabilizing hook. This is where the legendary abs must kick in, keeping the torso tight until you can get set up on the higher holds. You'll often see a climber simply collapse at the middle and sag off the rock. Whenever you can keep the hook while thrusting for higher holds, make certain to do so.

It's the much more secure technique, even if it's not always possible.

The aim here is to let those legendary abs hold you in check until you can get established on the next holds, where you can secure another hook to ease the load.

HANDS

Hands, arms, shoulder movement and body position all blend into one equation on overhanging climbs. The climb dictates what handholds you use, and most climbers differ on preferred grips – some favor to crimp the holds (claw grip); others favor a cling grip (open palm). The actual hold usually favors one grip over another. When you've a choice, the type of grip used often depends on strength, and how much bouldering a climber does (the bouldering ace often prefers the crimp). One usually can apply more crank using a crimp, but this grip tends to be more strenuous. And while the cling grip (open palm) is in some instances less strenuous, it's also less secure. There is little to be said about the slew of other possible grips – pocket grips, pinches, etc. – save that the more you use your thumb, the more secure you probably will be.

Ideal hand position means the hands are never placed wider than the shoulders. Imagine that your shoulders form a boundary extending in to the rock. Whenever you reach outside this boundary, the process of climbing becomes much more strenuous. Normally, the upper

Twisting the body closer to the rock.

John Sherman photo

torso follows the hands, falling in line directly below them. Whenever you use holds that are widely spaced – if the holds are anything shy of buckets – the physics of the operation means your shoulders must crank overtime to accomplish the move. When you've a choice, go with holds inside the imaginary box formed by the breadth of your shoulders.

We have gone over the notion of hinging off the shoulder while pushing off a foothold or hook. Though hinging is the preferred, strength-saving technique, it is limited by the fact that hinging with straight arms limits your reach. Sometimes (or oftentimes, depending on the route) you must crank your torso into the wall, lockoff, then reach. The same rule that applies to all lockoff moves also applies here: Get the elbow to the lat. However, a lockoff on overhanging terrain means gravity will try to turn you sideways. Don't fight this tendency. Allow your body to twist slightly, letting the outside shoulder dip away from the inside, pulling hand. This is a much more natural position, and it's a far less strenuous way to get that elbow to your lat. Trying to keep your chest parallel to the rock face when locking off requires far too much strength, and actually is inefficient and out of balance. Most all body juking and torso twisting is aimed at finding a more natural posture. Finding that position helps you find the place where you can best use your lat muscles.

We also have talked about dead points and powerglides. With regard to these techniques, the same considerations apply on overhanging rock as on vertical terrain. But there is another form of dynamic that doesn't come into its own until the angle requires it, and that's the . . .

FULL-BLOWN DYNAMIC

A full-blown dyno roughly can be described as requiring part, if not all, of the body to become totally dislocated from the rock during the upward flight. A truly world-class dislocate dyno is perhaps the most outrageous, and rarest, move in climbing. Its execution greatly favors a heavily-muscled climber who can generate the requisite explosive boost, combining enough spring to slam-dunk a basketball with enough hoist to hurl himself up and off a pull-up bar. Because so few climbers can do either, most dislocate dynos are well below world-class length. World-class dead point and powerglide dynos are required on most genuine test pieces. World-class dislocate dynos are found almost exclusively on boulders, and their utility for sportclimbing generally is overstated. For instance, the Left Eliminator at Fort Collins, Colorado, is one of America's most famous boulder problems. It's considerably shorter than world-class length and first was done 25 years ago, yet the number of climbers who have bagged it on their first or second try can be counted on one hand – and many of America's best have tried. The point is, few if any climbs require the world-class dislocate dyno since so few people actually can do them. Still, dislocate dynos are becoming more common on overhanging routes, so it's worth our while to understand the fundamentals.

The Dangler

The most strenuous dynamic is the one started with the feet already dangling. Say you're hanging on the lip of a roof, and the next hold is a knob three feet above you. You can't mantel on the lip – your only hope is to fire for the knob. That means you must generate enough boost to hurl yourself three feet, straight up. Clark Kent would be hard-pressed to do so using only his arms. The trick is to bring the lower body into play.

The standard technique is this: Get your hands situated on those spots from which you can generate the best hoist. Hanging from straight arms, gently swing the lower body – in and out. When the feet swing out perhaps two feet past the vertical point, or whatever feels right, it's time to fire. Remember that as you swing, the torque on your hands changes: the more you swing out, the less secure your grip

is, so you don't want to swing more than is necessary. In short, as the legs swing inward, prepare yourself. As they start to swing back out, start to initiate the hoist with the arms, simultaneously using the momentum of the swinging legs to aid the upward movement. On longish dynamos, you may even draw your legs up and immediately extend them again in a controlled little kicking move (in gymnastics, this is called kipping). It's all a matter of momentum and timing. Once you start to fly up, the common mistake is to stop yarding with the arms. This can leave you short of the mark. Keep cranking, and even at the dead point, when your free hand lets go to flash up for that knob – particularly at this point – keep trying to chuck that handhold to the ground. Keeping constant power on the initial holds (power point) means when you do latch that knob, you won't have to shockload it because you stopped cranking on the lower holds.

Everything previously mentioned about dynamics applies here as well: Try to get sufficient height to hit the hold with a slightly bent arm – since that way the muscles already are kicked in – then hit the hold with a ready grip, not just a slapdash hand. Precise timing on when to flash the hand up – realizing your dead point – is essential. As mentioned, some people find that by dropping the head it is easier to generate good air. This means as you fly upward, you must glance quickly up, lock your eyes onto the hold, and hit it perfectly with the reaching hand. Personally, I always try to keep a good bead on the lunged-for hold, finding it easier to hit a bulls-eye when I'm looking at it. If there's a decrease in hoisting power by keeping my head upright, I simply kip and yank a little harder. How and when you look at the goal is a matter of personal preference. Note that many pitchers glance away just before throwing home the pitch, and they don't seem to throw more than the usual number of bean balls.

John Sherman cranks a full-blown dynamic: Sink low once (don't pump up and down), press with the legs, pivot about the handhold, and try to keep at least one foot on (though this may require using a foothold higher than seems appropriate).

John Sherman photos

Double Mo

Far and away the most outrageous move in climbing – and the most infrequently used – is the two-handed dynamic dislocate. This is truly throwing yourself from one hold to another, so that at one point, the body loses contact with the rock altogether.

The double mo rarely is used unless the thrust holds are good ones, and the lunged-for holds, or hold, is so poor that you cannot hang onto it with only one arm. In extremely rare situations, the two-handed mo is the only way to span a huge section of rock – say four feet across. Here, both the thrust and lunged-for holds must be good ones. Only two times in 20 years of climbing have I had to use this technique on an actual route, and they were the most spectacular moves I've ever done.

The double mo is a game of power and timing. We've all seen the female gymnasts flying between the uneven parallel bars. They accomplish this by generating momentum off the lower bar (the power point), heaving on it until their shoulders are well above it. The trick that makes this rock move different from other forms of dynamics is that you must release the power point *before* you reach the dead point. That is, you unlatch and swoop both arms up while you are still accelerating up. The goal is for both hands to latch the higher hold at your dead point. Timing and accuracy must be perfect. And both arms must be pre-cocked so you can cling like a gila the moment you hit that upper hold. Best to experiment on boulders. Too much theoretical talk can only confuse the issue. It's pretty sketchy to try this technique on a route before you've mastered, or at least are familiar with, its nuances. It's definitely the hardest technique in climbing. But, since the two-handed mo is so infrequently used, it's more of a novelty than a practical skill. It's certainly fun to know how to do, though. To see someone uncork a really long two-hander is pretty amazing viewing.

STRATEGY

Strategy on overhanging routes does not differ significantly from that for vertical climbs – you study the topo, get the low-down (beta) from friends, eyeball the route, reduce the sections between visible 'good' holds, etc. There are but a few additional points worth mentioning. Perhaps the best strategy is to heed the techniques we've laid down, plus those that several world-class climbers will add at the end of this chapter. Beyond that, the most important consideration – one that absolutely can be decisive on overhanging routes – is pace.

(opposite)
Isabelle Patissier on the finals route, Snowbird, Utah.

Beth Wald photo

No matter what your level, once you start approaching your technical boundary, the limiting factor is strength. For everyone. What makes overhanging climbing unique among sports (and tricky to understand) is that two different types of strength are required. Obviously, you need good

endurance, or staying power, to make it up an overhanging route of any length. But good staying power alone won't get you over the crux – you need explosive strength for that. However, you have only a limited amount of explosive strength, and once you use it, your staying power is greatly reduced.

Though the correlation is an inexact one, let's look at another sport to try and understand this complex notion. In long-distance kayak racing, the strategy is to never go so fast that you go 'anaerobic.' Simplified, anaerobic is the state in which your body uses more oxygen than you can suck into your lungs. Once you get that paddle moving like a bee's wing, you quickly go into this oxygen-debt state and the only way to recover is to stop, or to paddle so slowly that you'll see nothing but the other competitor's backs for the duration of the race. In a long race, you'll often see the leader put on short bursts in an attempt to get those trailing to paddle so hard that they'll go anaerobic trying to catch up. Those that fall victim to this strategy essentially eliminate themselves from the race. With overhanging climbing, the same kind of fizz-out can occur. The harder you work on the easier sections, the less explosive strength you'll have, and once you tap heavily into your explosive strength, your staying power is so reduced that you'll have to contrive a rest or you'll quickly burn out and pitch off. Consequently, it is essential to use the least amount of strength on each section. You never want to power over a section if you can ease your way over it using heel hooks and straight arms. You want to climb at a pace that requires minimum effort – quickly here, slowly there, resting here, etc. Pace, then, is all about conserving both your endurance and explosive strength.

Knowing when to rest and when to carry on is crucial. Much of this comes from your ability to read your own body, from knowing its capabilities and limitations. When you can stick an entire leg into a hole and let go with both hands, obviously, you can stop and rest. But the game is rarely that black and white. You must ask yourself some questions: Will stopping at this particular hold result in recovery or even greater fatigue? Are you actually making the climb harder by trying to stop? Will you have enough gas to climb the crux if you don't stop somewhere soon? These questions, and a dozen more, must be answered on each overhanging route – when to climb fast, when to pause and study the rock overhead, when to really speed over a stretch, when to chalk, when to stop altogether. Once the climbing really gets grim, you rarely have the option of stopping at all. All your concentration must be focused on climbing the route. You either make it, get stumped by a move and pop, or burn out trying.

What further complicates the issue is the question of how hard is 'hard?' It's really a relative term. The strategies used by a 5.14 climber on a 5.14 route will be slightly different than those used by a 5.9 climber trying to bag a strenuous

5.9 route. The 5.9 route will require far less explosive strength, and will most likely be more of an endurance test than a matter of executing impossibly hard moves. With these mid-range routes, pacing and propitious resting are fundamental to success. On world-class test pieces, it's technique, experience and explosive strength all the way. If you were to take the very crux off a world class-route and paste it onto a boulder, many active climbers would be able to do it. The fact that a grim crux is preceded and followed by bleak terrain is many times what makes the big-name routes so formidable. Here, it's a matter of the climber having an abundance of explosive strength – built up through years of climbing and training – and the shrewd conservation of that strength through good pacing.

NO CAN FLASH

Once the route approaches your technical limit, your chances of being able to climb it on your first try decrease. On a rugged overhanging route, there are so many decisions to make that your odds of making all the right ones – the first time – are remote. That's why it's 'news' when somebody flashes a really hard route. Ordinarily, trial and error is used to work these climbs out. As you keep repeating the first section, moving progressively upward, you'll work out the best strategy for each section – how best to execute the moves, when to rest, when to go like hell. That first bit will get easier because of your familiarity with it, requiring less work to scale and leaving you with more reserves for the challenges ahead.

The value of having to siege a climb is that you quickly get an education on how to go about your work. You learn what works best for you, what your strengths and limitations are, and how to work with them. The point is, regardless of your level, it is worth your time to try to work out a difficult climb. Provided the route is not dangerous, go ahead and spend an afternoon falling off it. You'll probably learn more that afternoon than you would in a year of cruising routes well within your limits.

FALLING

When you pitch off an overhanging route, you drop like a stone. Unless you're climbing a genuine roof, you run the very real risk of swinging back into the wall and smacking it. Accordingly – and especially on routes in the 110-degree range – once you go airborne, you immediately must get braced for the impact. The technique is basic and needs no exhaustive study. Get your feet out. You don't want to lead with your head. Juke your body around so you swing into the wall straight on, hitting it feet first with the legs slightly bent and ready to absorb the jolt, like shock absorbers. Whatever you do, do not start flailing, pawing the air, losing it altogether. Appraise the fall before you commit yourself to

Mike Waugh takes a peel
in the Owens Gorge.

Kevin Powell photo

the climb, and be prepared if the fall comes. Provided your ropework is in order, keeping your head together is your best insurance against injury.

There is the chance your foot will get entangled in the line. If that happens during a fall, you'll get twirled around or hung upside down – it's a function of how your weight impacts the pro. Always be aware of where the rope is running as you climb. Try to keep it between your legs, never allowing it to run on top of your leg or around your side.

In summary, let's listen to what several experts have to say about overhanging face climbing. Hans Florine, who spends more time upside down than otherwise, says:

"No one is strong enough to hang out on their arms all day. You've got to read the moves and execute then decisively.

"With onsight climbing, when you hope to do the route on your first try, you must have faith both in the accuracy of the rating (of that route), and your ability to flash it. If you're on a 5.8 route that's well within your limit, but find yourself pumped out, you usually can pull up, lockoff, reach around above, and most likely your hand will slip into a pocket or onto a jug big enough for you to carry on. The most common disclaimer you'll hear about overhanging routes is: 'I would have made it had I seen that hold a second earlier.' Often on overhanging rock, you can't see a hold, especially a pocket, until you've pulled up to it, or even past it.

"Body position is key to conserving energy and strength on overhanging rock. You've got to keep your arms straight when resting – or trying to rest. When moving up, try to avoid locking off the holds. Move up by pushing with your legs and rotating your arms using your shoulders. You'll quickly pump out if you just crank up the route bent-armed, as you would climb a Bachar ladder. By working your feet up and rotating your shoulders like clock arms, it's possible to bring a side pull from over your head all the way to your stomach without ever bending your elbow. Often, backstepping one foot can twist your torso closer to the rock, allowing you to rotate up on one arm with far less effort.

"You'll do a lot of toe pointing on overhanging routes, so a low-top shoe is recommended."

Scott "Coz" Cosgrove is a low-profile climber who has established some of the hardest routes in the United States. A demon on the overhangs, Scott adds these valuable insights:

"Concentration, fluid breathing, simplicity of movement, sequence memory and a do-or-die tenacity for hard flashes are your basic ammo for overhanging climbing. Advanced routes further require the precision footwork of a high-wire walker, the rhythm and loose hips of M.C. Hammer and the ability to snatch holds like a frog tongues its prey.

"Many times your purchase – what holds you onto the overhang – is the counter-pressure of opposing hands and feet – i.e., right hand pulling, left foot hooked, and visa-versa. Remember that most toe and heel hooks are much more secure when you pull a little with the leg. Keep an eye out for hooks, but don't waste time and energy trying to have both feet set all of the time. Dangling a foot actually can help stabilize you. If opposing hand and foot placement is impossible, try crooking your free foot and leg under your planted foot to correct your balance.

"Learning to dyno is hard, but two tricks have helped the Coz. First, always try to latch the lunged-for hold at your dead point, when you're weightless. Second, focus your concentration and energy on your thrusting handholds – your 'power point.' For super long dynos, you might have to keep your head down at the start of the lunge, then look up and grab the hold while in flight. Focusing on the hold at the start makes aiming easier, but the upright head adversely affects your balance and cuts your vector, resulting in limited height. This peek-a-boo dyno requires plenty of practice to master, however.

"Resting and simplifying moves are much the same thing. Your arms have limited fuel, so don't waste it with unnecessary lock-offs, fancy footwork or climbing with bent arms or crooked shoulders. I find that hanging from holds with open palms is less strenuous than crimping. Crimping, like slow, static movement, should be used only when necessary. Climb like an inchworm: Place your hands and bring your feet up in one motion; thrust up to the next holds and, whenever possible, latch with open palms (open grip) and straight arms; then bring the feet up immediately and repeat the process.

"When resting on holds, I count to 30, resting each limb in turn. Depending on the holds, I'll sometimes repeat the process two or three times, concentrating on pumping the blood back into my arms. Knowing when to rest and when to pump it out is crucial; only experience can tell you when and where to try and recover, and when to keep on keeping on.

"You need a relaxed mind when the going gets rugged, and this is impossible without maintaining controlled, natural breathing. The best climbers never hold their breath, though this is common with novices. To maximize that relaxed attitude, breathe deep and hold each breath for a half-second; then exhale fully, blowing out carbon dioxide and thinning the lactic acid – the burn – in your limbs.

"Since rhythm and looseness are a must, I lug a boom-box to the cliff, plug in a little MoTown and keep it cranking till I'm into my groove. Go with familiar tunes to keep your concentration.

"Best results come when you don't tie your personal happiness to success or failure on a route. If you ever approach a route with a climb-it-at-all-costs attitude, you've made yourself a slave to success, which creates undo pressure and torpedoes your ability to relax, focus and, above all, enjoy yourself. Relax, crank hard, turn anxiety into raw power.

"Finally, leave the hemp and booze at the pad. Better yet, pitch them into the dumpster. You need a clear mind to analyse and execute your line. When I try to flash a route, I climb it many times in my mind, conceiving two or three probable strategies. To do this, I need a clear mind, not one addled by drug or drink.

"Climbing overhangs is itself the best practice. Try to learn one thing at a time, instead of baffling yourself with information overload. Move quickly and naturally, stay loose and focused. Good luck!"

Russ Walling is an ace climber who disdains anything but steep routes. Some of his philosophies differ considerably from those of other climbers. To get another opinion, let's listen to Russ:

"Paddling around on the slabs is good fun for you and your date, but the steep stuff is where it all happens. Once the angle and severity increase, so do the demands on the climber. Picture a climber on a 120-degree wall, dangling from an eighth-inch acorn, one foot epoxied to an atom-sized nubbin, struggling with a desperate clip. That is no slouch up there, rather a highly-specialized athlete. He probably tips

the scales at about 123 pounds wringing wet, but his mitts
are like vice locks. Yes, world-class strength is a good friend
to have; but sharp technique has landed countless more
climbers at the top of big-number test pieces than power
alone.

"You need experience, and you'll only find that on
overhanging rock. However, said rock need not be desperate
or committing. The boulders are the ultimate training
ground for building up a library of moves directly applicable

Scott Cosgrove dangles
in Joshua Tree: "Desert
Shield," 5.13b.

Bob Gaines photo

John Sherman rests on cocked arms while surveying the distant summit.

John Sherman photo

to overhanging routes. Rock is rock. Every hold you grab can teach you something about balance, personal limits and methods. Bouldering is invaluable because some of the best routes are little more than boulder problems found in the middle of a pitch.

"Every hold has a best way to grasp it. Use it wrong and you're off. Use it right and you're rewarded with another hold just as demanding. Link the series of holds perfectly and the summit is yours. The key is to find what feels most positive on the hold, then forget about it and begin to pull. Much energy is wasted fretting over a handhold, milking it, then, with failing strength, trying to pull on something that now feels crappy. Pop! – you're gone. If you simply had grabbed the hold, clasped the best part and pulled through, chances are you'd be on your way to the summit instead of hanging in your harness, bitching about how greased the hold was. You made it greasy with all the cocking around. Grab it and move.

"When you're satisfied that your hand has found the optimum grip, the pulling begins. If you're climbing statically, it's usually straightforward. You seek out holds above, then pull the hold down to around your peck, lock it off and repeat the process. It is important not to change the angle of your hand once you've clasped the hold. If it feels good with your wrist low and near the rock, keep it there. When your hand angle changes relative to the rock, so does the force on your fingers, and that often makes the hold less positive.

"Each pull with your arms should be complimented by thrust with your legs. Push, pull, lockoff, reach and fluidly repeat the process. You're wasting energy if you're pulling up, locking off, *then* trying to land your feet somewhere. Combined use of hands and feet will keep enough gas in your tank to allow a peek at the summit.

"On overhanging rock, footwork has been taken to a fine art. Every boot manufacturer offers some sort of precision-fitted, helium-weighted, drooped-toe, Ginsu-soled, atomic ballerina, big-name climber Signature Model climbing shoe. All the hype does actually aid the name of the game – footwork. Each foothold has a best spot on which to stand on. Most often, you place your toe or heel on overhanging rock, but be creative and never rule out the unorthodox – the outside edge, the instep, anything that works. Again, the key is to find it, set it, and move on. If it sticks, you're a hero. If you keep fretting over it, pawing endlessly at the face for exemplary purchase, you're as good as through. And just because it's a foothold doesn't mean it will be found at your feet. If you visit Hueco Tanks, for instance, heel hooks located over your head are your saviors. Think of hanging on a pull-up bar above a pool of hungry gators. Which would you rather have? Greasy palms and them gators nipping at your heels, or a leg up over the bar as you taunt Wally with a free hand. Point is, anytime you can take weight off your arms, do so!"

Whether the inimitable John Sherman is known better as a fabulous climber or a Homeric wise-acre is debatable. For a decade, his frequent articles have informed, entertained, and occasionally revolted the American climbing audience. No solemn dink, the following ingot was prefaced with this quip:

"Yo, Largo! Here's the piece on climbing overhangs I promised you. I trust you won't have so much trouble on them after reading it . . . .

"Overhangs force weight onto the arms, and even with quick movement, one's arms can swell like dirigibles. Without good footwork, creative resting and/or extensive training, the result can be Hindenbergian. So, the most important thing is to keep as much weight over the feet as possible. Keeping your feet on an overhanging wall requires great abdominal strength. When only one foot is on the rock, the dangling leg should be used as a counterbalance and often will assume radical, magazine-ad positioning.

"High footholds often are a good choice. They are easier to reach – provided you have the flexibility – and provide a support point closer to your center of gravity. On overhangs under 120 degrees, one sometimes can place a foot on a positive, waist-high hold, then sit on the heel, much like the rest position aid climbers (who?) use in etriers. This posture takes a lot of weight off the guns and allows the use of Lilliputian handholds.

"On overhangs beyond 120 degrees, heel hooking is often used. These hooks work best when the heel is above your center of gravity. Frequently, a heel is hooked above the hands. Try to get as much weight as possible on the heel, and if a heel-toe jam can be found, so much the better ('sticky' rands are a boon here). Heel hooking below one's center of gravity is effective when the hook is secure enough to pull outward from the wall. This taxes the hamstrings, but can provide an effect similar to the high foothold/aid climbers rest.

Get your hips over the lip of an overhang to help weight your feet.

John Sherman photo

"Even with footwork like Fred Astaire, one's arms still will have to support some weight. This is best managed with straight arms. With the skeletal system bearing the weight, only hand and forearm strength is needed to hang on. Expert climbers actually can rest in this straight-armed attitude, shaking out until they regain sufficient gusto to move on. When moving, remember to let the legs push the body up, using the arms only to keep the torso close enough to the wall to reach the next hold. When the holds are well spaced, using straight arms is, of course, impossible. If the footholds are there, go with a full lockoff, with hand next to shoulder, and chest sucked into the wall. Any arm position between straight and full lockoff quickly will gobble up your strength (a few seconds experimenting on a pull-up bar will verify this). Move fast in these situations.

"Body twists can allow long reaches on severely overhanging rock while keeping the arms straight. By twisting the upper body so that the shoulder axis becomes perpendicular to the rock, the hand supporting the climber's weight ends up low – below the opposite armpit, or lower still. This supporting arm remains straight and is crossing the chest and stomach. The reaching arm can be extended now, in a line parallel to the supporting arm, to reach the next hold. This technique utilizes the trunk muscles. Good holds are a must. On rare occasion, dire circumstances or the urge to show off forces one to climb on the arms alone. Here, use both arms to pull up, only releasing one when grasping the next hold. 'Kipping' – a deliberate and often natural pulling up of the knees – can help establish upward thrust while kicking the gut muscles in to assist the lats, shoulders and guns.

"When the arm's hydraulics aren't up to statically cranking a move, lunging comes into play. 'Dead point' refers both to the space between a sportclimber's ears, and the apex of his lunge, when the body is momentarily weightless. That's when you'll want to grab the lunged-for hold. Often, climbers will opt for dynamic moves over static ones, so they can move faster and conserve energy. When lunging, let the legs do as much of the work as possible. Think of the hands only as a pivot point about which the body will rotate up to the next hold. Set the feet well, sink low, then push with the legs. Let's not see any of this one, two, three, pumping-up-and-down jive before lunging. This just wastes energy and pumps up one's doubts. Sink down once and go!

"With the exception of wide cracks and employment, most climbers find roofs the most intimidating obstacles they come across. Arms remain straight as they usually don't have to pull up. Sticking under a roof (especially keeping the feet on) usually involves opposition techniques. Resting is usually impossible, so move fast.

"Wasn't that roof easy? Now you're at the lip, a thousand meters of bowel-loosening air beneath you – and the next six feet look bleak. Turning any lip is rough duty because the body hinges at the waist and the legs feel as though a Waimea undertow is sucking them back under the roof. Depending on the holds, surmounting said lip can involve a straight-on mantel, rocking over a foot hooked on the very lip, dragging oneself over on guns alone – even hucking a free-hanging, Clark Kent-dynamic for a higher hold. Whatever, getting the hips over the lip is critical and is most easily done with the hands as high above the lip as possible.

Manteling a lip with no handholds above.

John Sherman photo

"Resting is key on long overhangs. (Unending endurance will only get you so far – five-figure contracts, etc.) Plan rests in advance by surveying the line and picking spots where you can see a possible rest. On overhangs, these spots will be jugs, jams, kneebars and over-the-head footlocks. Kneebars are the best bet for a no-hands rest on overhanging turf.

"Training for overhanging face climbing is best done on the boulders; technique and power are readily acquired there. Long traverses are tedious, but effective for building endurance. It's wrist curls in the gym that build Sherman-esque forearm endurance. The forearms always are first to go. Forget the finger boards – they just promote injury. A King Kong upper body will help on power moves, but might screw you when it comes to endurance and is no substitute for technique.

"Let the legs do the work, keep the arms straight, move fast, plan rests in advance, and don't ever give up!"

Arêtes

When two planes of rock converge to form a 90-degree corner, we have a textbook arête. In practice, however, arête-climbing occurs on any 'edge' formed by converging faces. Generally, the sharper, more pronounced the edge, the tricker the climbing. Since the face-climbing revolution in the early 80s, climbers have gone crazy on arêtes, producing novel and technically-demanding routes up vertical – even overhanging – 'outside corners.' These routes offer some of the most dramatic climbing found on cliffside, with the 'double exposure' – afforded by scaling the genuine edge – compounding the intensity and splendor of the expedition.

Each arête requires something different from the climber – sometimes straddling the edge itself, feet plastered high; changing sides several times in 10 feet; jack-knifing up both sides, hands clawing blindly around the corner; body-hinging; bar-dooring; heel-hooking to stay on. Yes sir, the possible sequences are infinite. To get the inside line, let's bend an ear to Troy Mayr, who has made a career of scaling bleak arêtes. Says Troy:

"Something to consider before starting out is on which side you should rack your gear. Many times, the climbing will take place on one side of the edge, leaving only one hand free to place the gear (on difficult arêtes, two-handed rests are unheard of). Other times, climbing around the corner is required, making placement more thought- (and pump-) provoking. Many times, you can figure out from the deck what side you'll predominantly be climbing on. So take your time, and inspect the route carefully from below.

"Arêtes usually are strenuous, so the key is to figure out the best sequence and execute it quickly, but with control. Once you start climbing, move fluidly. Constantly look (and feel) around the corner for hidden holds. If holds allow, it's often more efficient to switch sides for 10 feet, versus liebacking straight up the edge. Remember, there are two planes to climb on, so remain aware of each of them. Many times, the easiest sequence is involved, obscure and improbable-looking.

"Hesitating or hanging about can throw you off balance and instantly pump you out. Unless you easily can let go with one or both hands, all but short rests on arête climbing are ill-advised – they're probably 'sucker' rests, which only waste time and valuable energy. It's almost always better to keep moving.

"Heel, toe and calf hooks are invaluable aids to maintain balance, limit the 'hinge' effect, and, at least briefly, unweight your arms. Many arêtes are impossible without using these techniques. A tiny indentation on the blind side of the arête

(opposite)
Troy Mayr on
"Iconoclast," 5.13a

Ron Wolfe photo

can feel like a jug when your heel is hooked on it properly. So keep track of what your hands already have passed over – it might save you from barn-dooring off. Often, a hook can provide a quick rest to shake out an arm. On one first ascent I did – the incomparable Magnetic Pork – I was able to place a left-heel hook above my left hand, which enabled me to move the left hand up statically, thus avoiding a desperate dyno-slap. The move was possible without the high heel hook, but was twice as strenuous and so fried my bacon that, once done, I couldn't flash the climbing above. The heel hook was the key.

"Slapping most often is necessary to pass blank sections between holds. It also is useful when gravity and body position require you to hold on with both hands, but you must slap and latch before pitching off. Be aggressive and quick whenever you slap. Don't overcling, which will produce an insta-pump; but don't slap casually, either, because that can send you winging into space. Slapping is a dynamic maneuver, and you must make use of the dead point – that millisecond when your body is weightless. Preceding any slap, you (usually) must dynamically hoist your torso up and slightly in. At the dead point, a hand flashes up for the hold. Perfect timing is the key here – just like with hitting a baseball.

"On extreme arêtes, body position is critical for conservation of energy. Muscles not being used should be relaxed, but ready to spring. Relaxing muscles and conserving energy often means the difference between the summit and flight time. Use body position to your advantage. On steep and overhanging routes, keep your center of gravity (your hips) close to the wall and never try to force, or 'muscle,' your way up.

"Sometimes, you won't be able to stop and chalk up because your clutch on the arête is too desperate. In this

case, even the slightest wind can help keep your hands dry. Also, be aware of humidity, which can make hands sweaty. Colder weather is ideal for climbing arêtes. Skin and rubber friction increase dramatically when the temperature is below 55 degrees.

"The multi-dimensional nature of arête climbing provides exciting combinations of moves and intriguing problem-solving designs, both mental and physical. Good luck fighting the pump!"

Note that the heart of Troy's advice covers good body position, conservation of energy, relaxing when possible and climbing aggressively when need be, as well as the necessity for precise hand and boot placement. He also recommends scoping out the route thoroughly from the ground before roping up. By now, these ideas should be well-established as fundamental to all face climbing.

Arêtes present unique climbing problems. It's hard to directly contrast arête climbing with other modes of face climbing, and the person interested in becoming good at ascending arêtes should ease into the tournament. Most every crag presently has a slew of arête climbs. Start with the moderate ones, even if they're well below your normal standard. Becoming 'arête fluent' comes most readily through repeating the unusual body positions, the various hooking (toe, heel and calf) techniques and the strange and shifting balance problems. It's much like riding a bike: once you get the hang of it, you'll have the technique for life. Arête climbs almost always are exposed, committing and exhilarating. Likewise, these routes provide some of the most spectacular falls you'd ever hope to see – or take. Because of the constant liebacking and counter-pressuring, a leader can rifle off like he's spring-loaded, and oftentimes he does so quite unexpectedly. Such peelers provide all the more reason to ease onto the moderate ones before pushing your luck on the desperates.

Arête climbing is intriguing because often the protection is thin and problems cannot be muscled, resulting in more of a psychological than a physical challenge. Even a moderate arête can provide you with some of your most memorable moments. A 5.13 climber might well see God on a dicey 5.11 arête. 'Wild,' 'hairy,' 'mind-boggling' – all these are commonly-used terms to describe the really prime arêtes. Allow me an anecdote here:

At my home crag, there's a flawless, 400-foot arête that grabs your eye. For years we all talked about climbing it. Finally, Tobin Sorrenson did, though he traversed in above the first 100 feet, which were then too steep and slippery to climb in the old, case-hardened P.A.s. Shortly after the first sticky boots arrived, Dwight Brooks and I went up to look at climbing the entire arête. The first 60 feet were moderate, and gained an old bail-off bolt. The next protection was the first of Tobin's bolts, 40 feet above. The climbing looked spectacularly insecure, poised on the very edge of the steep, pearly arête. From the little stance at the bail-off bolt, I couldn't see a single foothold above, so once started, there would be no stopping or turning back. It looked like a slippery, pumping hinge job all the way, with an unthinkable fall if things went bad. Yet, it did look flashable. Before I considered the fall, I yelled down at Dwight to watch me close, then cast off.

Since the left wall was dead bald, I had both hands palming round the corner, and both feet pasted right up next to them, counter-smearing. Whenever I tried to pause, my boots started oozing toward the edge – a motion checked only by slapping my palm up and quickly shuffling my feet higher. Pausing or hanging from one hand to chalk was impossible. After about a dozen feet of unrelenting 5.11, I came to a point of no return. Like with most difficult arêtes, downclimbing was impossible. I probably could have jumped off, however, and staggered home needing only a few dozen skin grafts.

"Looking good," Dwight yelled up to me. I believed him, and carried on. After another 10 feet, Tobin's first bolt still looked a mile away. The edge felt greasier than the fries at Fatburger and my hands were slipping horribly on it. But there was no jumping now. Ten more feet, and I regretted ever having been born.

"Looking solid," Dwight yelled. Now, Dwight Brooks is 220 pounds of corded muscle. With a shock of brown hair and a jaw like a park bench, he cuts a striking figure. But his teeth are too straight and too white for an honest man and I didn't buy the bit about me looking solid. Never mind how I looked, what mattered was how I felt. And I still had 10 feet to go.

Technically, no single move was harder, or easier, than minimal 5.11. Very doable, yes, but the number rating ignored what I could not – the sounds of clinking pitchforks and the slavering minotaurs and legions of demons marching through my mind. Finally, I wobbled up to Tobin's first bolt, where part of me died to see that he'd placed that bolt off the most woeful edge, on a wee little scallop inches from the very corner, which appeared rounded and greasier than ever. I flashed on the story of Tobin, who had made a long, unprotected traverse to get here, and who had wept openly while placing this bolt. Gaping at that scallop, I knew why. I quickly hiked my leg up and set the outside edge of my boot on that scallop. My hands were pasted round the corner but were no help, ever ebbing off the polished and rounded lip. There was no other hand hold. With my knee jacked up by my chin, I was set up wrong for the move, and knew it. My only prospect was a virtual no-handed stand-up on that shitty little scallop, my body crooked sideways and out of balance, looking at an 80-footer.

Had my foot blown off that scallop I wouldn't be typing this now, but instead dictating it, in a whisper, flat on my broken back, with wires and conduits running from my vitals to hissing machinery on the walls. That very moment, executing that single high step, was my most intense in 20 years of climbing. And it all happened on a 5.11 route – hard, certainly, but miles from any top-grade test piece. Only on an arête . . . .

Modes of
Ascent

Prior to about 1975, there was only one way to climb. There were rare exceptions, but normally, you scaled the route on your first or second try. If you could not, and were a real hardhead, you'd give it a couple more tries. Otherwise, you rapped off and came back when you were feeling stronger. Flashing a route still is the preferred mode – that is, walking up to a route you have never seen before, putting on the rack and leading to the top, placing all the protection and not resorting to shenanigans. But this mode is an impossible and impractical one for really gruesome climbs. When the inconceivably hard climbs first were bagged, climbers were forced to start 'working' the route, spending days, even weeks, 'falling up' the cliff. Yet, even these days when anything goes, an ascent is not considered 'free' until the climber can scale the route, bottom to top, without falling. Sounds like a black-and-white affair, doesn't it? In practice, however, the means by which a climber eventually 'leads' the pitch may involve the most dazzling chicanery. That acknowledged, a loose set of terms have evolved that explain exactly what means were used. Even the most ardent hang-dogger won't argue that the means can make all the difference.

Look at it this way. I have a Japanese friend named Otani, who is one of the world's great adventurers. I first met Otani on the North Pole in 1989. If you peruse the logbook of the Polar Adventurers, you'll see both our names, alongside the names of 80 other hale folk who have made it to the top of the world. At a glance, our credentials would appear the same, for Otani and I both gained the Pole at virtually the same time. The fact is, however, that I flew most of the way there, then cruised the last miles on a 100-horsepower snowmobile, smoking cigars and drinking Aquavit. Otani had just spent the longest two months of his life battling north, bull-whipping 15 wayward curs, fleeing polar bears, braving melting ice, vicious storms and thin rations. So, you see, the means by which we both got to latitude zero tells two real, but separate tales – one of a remarkable adventurer, the other of a ringer who thieved his way onto the Pole and into the Polar Adventurer's hallowed logbook. The same disparities apply to many of the new-wave face climbs as well. What's important is how the climber went about his business.

Note that, while the end has often come to justify the means of ascent, the closer a climber comes to realizing the old ethics – to performing the on-sight flash – the more

(opposite)
Mari Gingery on
"Scirocco," California
Needles.

Greg Epperson photo

celebrated his effort is considered. So it's safe to say that the mode of ascent will remain important to climbers, as it should.

Russ Walling and I put our heads together and came up with the following thoughts on the various modes of ascent:

Onsight Free Solo

Angus MacGillicuddy has never been to Mt. Hogwash. Walking along the base, Angus spots a line of bolts up an overhanging schist intrusion. He fancies the look of the route, laces up his boots, blows his nose, chalks up and gapes at several girls from the Swedish Sport Climbing Team, who are limbering up and changing into bright-colored tights. Psyched, Angus winks, spits into his palms, then solos up the schist intrusion.

Free Solo

Angus has been to Mt. Roughage several times. On two occasions, he's climbed The Watercloset, a difficult route that follows a basalt intrusion via chancy dynamics. Angus has it in mind to solo The Watercloset. Now at the base, he laces up, touches his toes, exhales hard, then solos the route.

Worked Solo

Angus has been coming to Mt. Peatmoss for 11 years. He's lead Compost 50 times, toproped it 70 times, and, also on a toprope, has worked the crux bit over and over till he knows it better than the hair on his palms. Now he plans to 'solo' Compost, an intricate razor job up a monzonite intrusion. At the base, he flexes his guns, flexes his back, flexes his loins, jumps onto Compost and solos it in six minutes.

Mike Waugh hangdogging it on "LA Machine", Joshua Tree

Kevin Powell photo

Onsight Flash or a Vue

Angus has never been to Mt. Basura. One route, The Offal, takes a loose line up a steep albeit trashy intrusion. Angus racks up and leads The Offal straight off, placing all the gear. He takes no falls, nor a single rest on the line.

Beta Flash

This is Angus' first trip to Mt. Gismo. At the local pub, Angus runs into Jack Nastyface, the local hardman. Since Angus is buying, Jack describes down to the last pinky lock the sequence for climbing The Honest Indonesian, an improbable Mt. Gismo test piece following a sketchy dun intrusion. With the sequence memorized, Angus flashes the route the next afternoon.

(opposite) Daryl Nakihara on "Intruding Dike", City of Rocks, Idaho.

Kevin Powell photo

Deja Vu

It's been some years since Angus was last at Mt. Tallywhacker. He remembers trying the Chamfered Luby – and failing miserably. The successive lunges along the scarlet intrusion notwithstanding, he remembers little about the route. But Angus is a better climber than he was 7 years ago, and the next morning, he manhandles the Chamfered Luby on his 'first' try.

Red Point

Angus has tried to climb The Widget on Mt. Sputnik for five years now. He's aided it, toproped it, studied it from a helicopter, on jumars, with opera glasses. Finally, he leads it, no falls, placing the gear as he goes.

Pink Point

Angus has been trying to climb The Bullwhip on Mt. Maplethorp for 10 years. He's gotten close, and after hosing the Windgate intrusion with Gumout, squeegeeing it clean, then buffing each hold with 600-grit sand paper, he wants to try the lead once again. But first, he raps down the route, places all the gear, then flashes the lead.

Brown Point

Angus has never tried Intelligent Gas From Uranus on Mt. Bachar. He starts up the blank face between the two brown intrusions full of intentions to make a flash ascent. Things go bad in a hurry, and Angus soon is hanging from the cord. He's quickly on a toprope, pulling through the first two grim bits. Later, stumped at the crux, he incorporates a side rope, one etrier and a 'come-along' belay. This makes Angus feel like he's got the strength of 10 men as he works out the crux. Within hours, he stands on the summit, ready to rap down and place the gear for a 'pink point' ascent the next day.

There are other procedures that Angus sometimes employs in his quest for the summit that are worth mentioning. For instance, he's been known to 'hangdog.' That is, after he falls off his lead attempt, he won't hesitate to hang on the rope, rest, then carry on fully refreshed.

When Angus first went to Mt. Pipedream, he didn't have time for too many shenanigans, but he did want to bag The Tijuana Virgin, a nearly non-existent line of pockets along an ivory intrusion. To save time, he rapped down to the crux, worked it out on a toprope, then rapped to the deck and 'red pointed' the route. Thus, Angus had 'speed dogged' the route (also known as 'greyhounding').

At Mt. Cameltoe, Angus desperately wanted to scale The Man in the Boat, but first wanted the beta. He sent his hapless buddy – Shawn O'Sean – up to work out the moves, while he watched smugly from below. Shawn was 'seeing-eye dogging' for Angus, who was then set to try his Beta Flash.

Also at Mt. Cameltoe, Angus took a liking to The Pipefitter. He did not, however, like the looks of the first bolt, which was 30 feet off the talus. Angus needed a 'coon dog' to go up and fetch him that first clip. Shawn had already mounted The Pipefitter 69 times before, and gladly 'coon dogged' for Angus. He clipped the first bolt, lowered, then handed off the blunted sharp end for Rover to take over – in relative safety.

Angus encountered a similar situation at Mt. Hamstring. The Rocky Mountain Oyster followed an overhanging intrusion, and the first bolt, way the hell up there, already had a quickdraw on it. Nobody's fool, Angus took a long bight of rope, twirled it over his head like a lariat and hurled it at the in situ quickdraw. The bight of rope hit the dogleg carabiner at the gate and with a click!, Angus was clipped in! He named this method the 'rodeo clip.'

Angus certainly is not one, but he's known a few 'dog's asses.' These are craven swine who cannot accept defeat and alter an existing route to make it easier for them to scale, placing additional bolts, chiseling holds, etc. Starvation, thirst and financial ruin to them all.

Competition

There is some question about where the first climbing competitions took place. California climbers like to think that the annual bouldering competition in the Golden State, started in the late 70s, laid the groundwork for the big-time events of the 90s. It's more likely, however, that competitions evolved concurrently around the world. The Eastern European countries, particularly the Soviet Union, have held speed-climbing competitions for decades. However, there is no telling who was first to test for technical difficulty.

The first competitions were staged on real cliffs. But this format had all kinds of snafus. Weather was a continual problem, as was finding an appropriate trio of routes to serve as successive heats. Holds would break, nut placements would change after manifold falls, etc. The trend finally has settled – almost exclusively – on artificial walls, where the difficulty can be adjusted for progressive heats, and the steady flow of competitors controlled.

Staging one of these events is involved and expensive. Accordingly, the competitions are not mere showcases for the very best. Instead, for the most part, they have become sort of all-comers meets – as much fascinating social events as anything else. This is due to a shameful lack of sponsorship. American equipment manufacturers traditionally have been much more interested in bilking the climbing community for profit than in pumping even nominal funds back into the sport. There are exceptions, but without a lot of entry fees from casual contestants, competitions are economically unfeasible.

Yet, in one important sense, the open format of competitions is a blessing. The more people directly involved, the better the event. I don't think competitions would have taken off like they have if they were merely spectator events. Now, beginners, novices, intermediate climbers, et al. – any willing climber – can be part of the show. It's a good deal for all. In an era when different factions are squabbling over this and that, these competitions bring people together and help defuse otherwise petty differences. It's virtually impossible not to enjoy yourself at a well-staged event, what with all the screaming kids and unleashed dogs, the ass-kicking sound track, the buffoon working the microphone, and all your friends falling off the 5.10a route, which is probably closer to 5.11e. It's a riot.

Serious regional, national and international events generally are reserved for experts. But, as interest grows, look for some of these elite events to have an all-comers competition as well as the headline meet. The reasons for

(opposite)
World Cup competition at Nimes, France.

Beth Wald photo

this are simple. Climbers are, for the most part, action-oriented. Sure, it's entertaining to watch Rocket Cullpepper glide up the 5.14 route like it's a staircase; but if you've driven all the way from Amarillo, you'll want to sink your teeth into something more than the Power Bars that swarthy fellow is hawking on sidelines. Climbers want, and will come to expect, some action of their own. In the future, look for many meets, regardless of size and prestige, to have an open category for the willing. After all, it's the entrance fees that supply the prizes.

THE MEDIUM

Artificial walls and holds have evolved steadily over the last few years. The holds first were designed for use on practice walls. These evolved when weekend warriors built plywood 'cliffs' in their backyards, bolting on assorted bleak holds and staying tuned with a little after-hours hand-traversing. Soon, climbing shops built practice routes on storeroom walls, attracting customers and attention to the sport. Universities started building large-scale walls for physical education programs. Today, there are some impressive 'climbing gyms' in the works, which will combine weight-training facilities with the climbing walls. And recently, a whiskey distiller traveled the country with a few hotshot climbers and an artificial wall, promoting 'sportclimbing' and hard drink, and inviting passers-by to tie in and have a go. In short, sportclimbing has arrived. For better or worse, there is a whole cult of expert artificial wall climbers in places like Delaware and Key Largo, Florida, hundreds of miles away from the nearest cliff. Remarkably, some of these experts have never climbed on an actual crag!

Without the advent of these many sportclimbing mediums, the pre-fab panels and the incredible variety of artificial holds would not be nearly so refined. They're simply too costly to make for competitions alone.

THE WALL

The European competition circuit is promoted on a much grander scale than its American counterpart, so Europeans have more franks and deutsche marks to spend on custom-designed walls, some of which are not far from art in their structure and relief. In America, where climbing industry money is in shorter supply, competitions have been staged on all manner of structures, including the side of luxury hotels and backpacking shops. Most recently, competitions have opted for a less-permanent medium – namely, custom climbing panels lashed to construction scaffolds, with the ass-end of the whole rig anchored by a massive counter-weight to keep the wall static. These panels vary in size, but usually are about four feet square. They feature every conceivable type of hold – rounded nothings, underclings, side-pulls, comely jugs – the works. They also are machined to accept bolt-on holds, allowing each panel to be retro-fitted to whatever degree of difficulty the course setter desires.

A new and usually much bigger series of panels may soon replace the old ones. In particular, Carp, Entre Prises and JMB Sportclimbing Designs have come out with one-piece 'molded' panels so authentic in their rock-like relief that some climbers consider them better than the real thing! The holds are not bolted on but part of the mold; and some of these panels are bigger than four meters square. Whether a big rig full of these panels will hit the road like a carnival act, serving every nickel-and-dime local competition, seems doubtful. Economics and practical concerns most likely will relegate the use of these super panels to climbing gyms and big-time regional and international meets. Climbing difficulty is altered by changing the angle of the panel; unlike the traditional bolt-on units, these panels often offer more climbing options – move for move – than an actual cliff will.

A Typical Wall

There is no such thing as a typical wall. Every wall, like every climb, varies according to the designer and the available materials. However, there are several elements that you are bound to see.

Organizers love the overhanging stuff, so even novice routes are at least 90 degrees. The angle usually depends on the scaffolding configuration. As mentioned, rather than constructing a permanent wall, or tooling out the wall of an existing building, competitions are moving more to temporary rigs composed of the panels bolted to scaffolding. As each of the panels are hinged together, the climb tends to bulge in steps – for example, a vertical panel is followed by one 20 degrees overhung, followed by another vertical one, and so on. The super 'molded' panels notwithstanding, each panel is relatively small, the contestant continually is reaching and yarding his feet over a bulge, and this makes for very awkward and jerky sequences. You never can get established on a four-foot piece of 'rock,' so only a very diminutive chap would feel at home on such a route. Nevertheless, that's what you're looking at in many cases.

World Cup competition in Berkeley, California was built of climbing panels bolted to scaffolding.

Beth Wald photo

If the competition does not utilize panels, then you're dealing with some kind of edifice with bolted-on holds – most likely, the side of a building. Such routes make for more fluid climbing, owing to the consistent angle. But, considering the dozens of lag-bolts necessary to secure holds to a building, coupled with the boot marks of a hundred rabid climbers, most meet organizers are going with the scaffolding rigs and avoiding befouling their mortgaged buildings.

There are only a few definitive things I can say about the walls. No two will be the same. The angle will be dead vertical at the minimum – no slab climbing at competitions. Lastly, virtually all American competitions have done away with trying to replicate cracks – even short sections of crack climbing – so it's all face holds, and the rare sham lieback.

Holds

When first introduced, one could talk in specific terms about the bolt-on holds. These days, they come is such a variety and there are so many on the market that it's impossible to describe a "normal" bolt-on hold. Most are made using some type of resin base mixed with base grit. For the most part, even when they are caked with chalk, the purchase is equal to the gnarliest hold at Joshua Tree.

THE SET UP

Again, no two competitions are alike. Many now are opting to toprope competitors, rather than rig the wall for the simulated lead. Perhaps it's more exciting to see your buddy pay for his mistake by plunging off the wall; but should a competitor catch his toe on the cord, spin upside down and smack his bean on the wall, we'll all be losers. So look for the toprope in all but the expert meets.

Since competitions are geared toward determining technical proficiency, the idea that elapsed time should figure into things is questionable. If two climbers flashed the final climb, some early competitions determined the winner by the elapsed time. Not good, since both men and women climbed the thing; and to be eliminated because you were a fraction slower than Joe has led some victims to feel they'd been robbed — and rightly so. Accordingly, timing ascents has, for the most part, been done away with. Most often, if you flash the route, you advance. This system presents some problems, however. Competitions routinely run long, given the various heats. Sometimes there are hundreds of contestants. A recent solution, and perhaps the only viable one for a big event, is to give each contestant an allotted time to complete the route – not so little that it requires speed climbing, and not so much that one climber can hold up the show.

The first competitions were loose, ill-defined affairs fraught with scandalous judging and national prejudices. The UIAA, a European-based climbing organization now has a Competitions Committee (CICE) that makes rules for and oversees international competitions. In the United States, the member organization of the CICE is the American Sport Climbers Federation (ASCF), which in turn sanctions local, state, regional, and national competitions. In addition, the ASCF chooses a national team for representation at international events, and provides a training program for judges.

The ASCF focuses its efforts in two ways: sanctioning competitions for organizers, and providing a numerical ranking for climbers. Competitors gain points at local and regional competitions that allow them ultimately to compete for a place on the national climbing team. Such point ranking also allows potential sponsors of climbers to see how good they really are.

Membership in the ASCF is available at several levels. An individual who wishes to compete and gain standing can join for $25. Anyone with an interest in organizing or competing can reach the ASCF at 125 W. 96th Street, #1D, New York, NY, 10025.

Heats

Let's presume that the competition is an all-comers meet, since 80 percent of them now are. The first round will take place on a route considered doable for an active climber. Most first heat climbs are minimal 5.10 in difficulty. This usually trims the crowd in half. In the next heat, organizers probably will jack the difficulty up to mid-5.11 range, which prunes the competition down to a handful. The third and, most often, final heat always is dreadfully severe. Often, no one makes it to the top, and the winner is the one who got the highest.

To get an overview of the whole process, let's dial up Troy Mayr, who is rapidly becoming one of the premier course setters in the United States:

"Competition walls are built on either existing structures, like the side of a building, or constructed piece by piece on a temporary scaffolding. Climbs on buildings are usually topped by an 'obstacle,' generally a fiberglass or plywood roof that is lashed to the top of the route. Otherwise, it's vertical climbing all the way. Scaffolding walls can be built to most any specs, and the angles are as radical as the course setter desires. Climbs put on buildings are rock solid; the holds are bolted straight onto the concrete. Scaffolding climbs, however, are prone to flexing since the artificial panels must support body weight with little or no central support: only the corners are lashed or bolted down. The smaller or thicker the panels, the less they will flex. However, the works have to be notably loose to adversely affect a climber's performance.

"Both modes of competition climbs can be fashioned in or out of doors. Outdoor walls entail the same concerns found at the crags. Will it rain? Is the wall in the sun, and if it is, for how many hours and at what time of day? Most often, the course setter has, or should have, taken these factors into consideration and insured an impartial arena. However, sometimes these concerns cannot be managed because of logistical restraints, so be prepared. Indoors, of course, these types of problems are inconsequential. Instead, the handicaps include increased humidity and the normally hot and intense lighting. But, everyone must struggle with the same problems, resulting in parity.

"Unless the competition is staged in an official arena, there are considerable height constraints on a wall's size. Most indoor competitions feature walls at, or under, about 30 feet in height. Overall, competition walls vary from 20 to 100 feet. The average wall is about 30 feet tall for regional/local competitions, and 60 feet for national/international competitions.

"There are many variables that affect how a course will be set. First, one must consider how well a wall will allow the retrofitting of holds – that is, how easy and fast can the holds be changed? It ranges from the relatively easy – screwing holds into pre-existing holes – to breaking out the masonry drill for each hold – an epic and time-consuming task. Also, things can and do go wrong, even with painstaking planning – wrong tools, stripped bolts, inherent wall engineering snafus, a lack of time, it's 10 minutes till the competition begins, etc. Any or all of these problems make the course setter's job a tough one.

"Designing a course often is as taxing as climbing the same. Generally, you want to fashion a route that gets progressively more difficult without forcing everyone into a fall at the same place. You must take into account factors like reach, men and women climbers and the desires of sponsors and judges, while trying to feature a panoply of moves including dynos, thin stuff, tricky bits, gorilla cranks, Frankenstein liebacks, et. al. Usually, the course setter is faced with at least one ongoing nightmare – like when it's three o'clock in the morning and the power goes down. When this happens, the course setter usually is trashed from climbing 2,000 feet on the wall while working out the sequence. Many artificial walls aren't 'meet ready' until sunrise, if that early. Time, or the lack of it, is a constant problem. Most competition walls require expensive rental equipment (scaffolding, lights, etc.), as well as space fees, so the essential 'extra' days needed to properly set the course usually don't exist. For the most part, course setting is a thankless job. Though he can literally make or break a competition, a course setter's only solace is to either kick back and reap the praises of a gem route, or endure the tongue lashings of a bad one.

"When I set a course, my decisions are based on many of the factors mentioned above, as well as any special requests of the event promoter and sponsors. At one competition, I was asked to create an "exciting' course for both spectators and climbers. Thus, the course consisted of a number of power moves topped by a full-on, double dislocate dyno to the 'summit' Generally, I try to create a highly visual, move-aesthetic course. If at all possible, I take into account natural conditions. If the wall is in the sun and it's humid and greasy, I'll skip the slopers and tweakers and go with more positive holds and ingenious sequences – like side pulls and underclings. It's always good to throw in a jumbo dyno somewhere as well, even if it's jug to jug. In cool, shady conditions, I'll strive for hard sequences, but might include a few dime cranks and some pumping slope jobs as well. If the wall is long – say, over 40 feet – it probably will involve more spread-out moves, as opposed to crunch work, which is used to maximize limited wall space. Overall, most courses get increasingly difficult and pumping as you go higher. Often, I will devise a tricky, but effective rest position somewhere on the wall, so when competing, be aware of this possibility. Any experienced course setter will factor in the weather and natural conditions, as well as strive after fun moves, install a really spectacular sequence somewhere, try to build in a requisite pump sequence, and not try to bust a climber's chops by requiring little dime pulls at the crux. All of these things should help a competitor second-guess the decisions of the course setter. Also, if you know what kind of climbing the course setter favors, you're bound to see his pet techniques employed on the course.

"If the competition entails simulated leading, expect to get a semi-rest at some of the clips. No doubt there will be some hard clips as well, but not every clip will be a desperate one. This allows a competitor little step-by-step goals – keeping the confidence up – as opposed to the one big goal of reaching the top.

"The competitors generally don't affect my decisions when I'm designing a route. Nor do I strive after a certain rating. I concentrate on eliminating 'X' number of people per round, ultimately terminating all but one – the winner.

"In the future, walls be better engineered, allowing design of more spectacular routes for both climbers and spectators. Also, as more money is available, events will be better organized and less rushed, allowing more time to both set courses and compete. Categories will expand. Speed climbing will become more popular, and rehearsed difficulty – worked routes – will take the spotlight. Competitors will be younger (as in gymnastics competitions), but experience will favor the older, stronger climbers (as in surfing contests). Ultimately, colleges and schools will have climbing teams, and local, regional and national competitions will be much more structured. Good luck!"

PREPARATION

Briefly, the best preparation for climbing on artificial walls is to climb artificial walls. The climbing resembles actual rock climbing, of course, but it differs enough that someone familiar with ascending artificial walls (with or without bolt-on holds) has a distinct advantage over someone who isn't. Those serious about competition often construct hand traverses – using the artificial holds – in their backyards, and practice regularly on them. In many areas, climbers have constructed 'urban crags' by bolting holds onto convenient walls or bridges – even onto the undersides of freeway overpasses. One area in Pasadena, California, is host to concrete climbs upwards of 60 feet tall. Spending time on these artificial structures not only keeps your fingers tuned for the crags, but will familiarize you with the feel of competition walls. And avoiding the authorities, who want to know who the hell bolted all that crap onto state property, also can add some thrill to the venture.

With the exception of 'elite' competitions, any prize money is so nominal that the sport could hardly be called a professional industry. Even the best competitive climbers in America have to chase their tails trying to make a go of it. Equipment manufacturers will latch onto a champion like a cancer, squeezing every drop of promotional value from him or her; but rarely do they pay "their" climber substantial green money. For you and me, it's best to consider the whole thing an amateur sport. If you win a rope, or a couple hundred bucks, great. If you don't, there's still no excuse not to enjoy yourself. And that should be the goal for anyone interested in competing. Go to have a good time. Don't fret if you pitch off on the first heat. There will always be another competition.

I can't tell you how to compete, or how to be a champion, if that's what you aspire to. There are, however, a few common considerations that can optimize your performance.

First, most often, you have to jump right on the wall and perform, and the first moves are bound to be stiff. Make sure to warm up. Stretch, hang on the scaffolding, from a door jamb – hang on anything – to get limbered up and get your fingers ready. Keep limbering up till it's your turn to climb.

Second, don't power down a six-egg omelet, a dozen flapjacks, bangers, hash browns, a couple of bear claws and a ten cups of jo and expect to feel prime on the overhanging wall. Go easy on the grub, but not so spare that you feel depleted. Many climbers go with quick-energy bars or carbo drinks shortly before their heat, getting the volts without the bulk. (Mind you, each competition has a handful of dead-serious competitors who look like they've just survived 50 days at sea in a life jacket. With .00002 percent body fat, their keen faces drawn and pinched, you hope they win so they can finally enjoy a square meal.)

While competitions are an ever-evolving affair, the previous info should put you in decent standing, regardless of the competitive format. Like any competition, the climber who has competed a lot has a decided advantage over someone with the same ability whose competitive experience is less extensive. If you have aspirations towards serious competition, travel far and wide and enter as many meets as possible. You'll learn something valuable from each one.

While few of us go to these events with even remote hopes of winning, let's be honest enough to admit that we'd rather make a good showing than a poor one. To that end, let's pick the minds of those who have competed at the big meets, and see if we can't get a small edge over the rest of the competitors.

First, let's listen to Hans Florine, speed-climbing champion and rising competitive climber.

"Competition climbing is more of a mental game than sportclimbing at the crags. You have to block out all the crowd/announcer racket, concentrate, execute hard gymnastic moves, plus deal with the pressure of being 'on the spot.' If you blow a move and slip, you're out of there – you cannot lower and try again. Under these circumstances, it might be better to be a little nervous and really focused than to be utterly relaxed and calm.

'Things to contemplate in isolation before competing: Remember, 'the route goes.' You must assume that the course setter designed the route so it will go, and you have to believe you're as good or better a climber than the course setter. Visualize clipping that last quickdraw or climbing the entire route and topping out.

"When warming up, *do not* get involved with other competitors (especially those better than you) in a bouldering contest on the warm-up wall. The quickest way to get rid of competition is to have them dyno for some one-finger pocket. Don't laugh. I've seen it happen. Everyone takes a different amount of time to recover. I try to get my forearms fully pumped on the warm-up wall then have at least an hour's rest before getting on the competition wall. However, you should warm up your fingers just before getting on the competitive route.

'Things to remember while on the route: On 'artificial rock,' the sequences are more limited than on the crags. With that in mind, I try to quickly pump through the moves, rather than hanging out to scope them. If you're at a genuine resting place, where you can momentarily de-pump, then snatch a quick look at the rest of the climb. But always be looking above, figuring out the next sequence. If the rest is marginal and you see a probable sequence above, go for it. You'll probably do better than if you hung out running sequences through your head, getting all the more tired before trying the moves. If the competition involves simulated leading, remember that the course setter wants you to make the clip, so count on a moderate rest, or a pause, at each quickdraw. If the clip feels awkward and strenuous, climb a little higher until it feels easier.

"Above all else, know the rules before you get on the route! Know how much time you have to complete the route. Know what is on and off the route. On some routes, panel edges may or may not be used. And some of the routes I've climbed have allowed climbers to grab the bolts!"

Alison Osius, senior editor of *Climbing*, is a member of the U.S. Climbing Team and a proven performer on the international circuit. Her competitive experience is principally with elite meets, but her counsel is germane to any competition.

"All 'plastic' climbing has much in common, so spend time on practice walls and learn what to expect. You're always learning, and storing up tricks you can later use for a competition. Generally, the moves are more straightforward than on rock: holds stand out and the options are fewer. Learn the common moves, like the 'flag,' where a free leg passes behind the set leg and extends out behind you close to the rock as a counterbalance. This helps check the barn-door effect, while at the same time placing your weight more squarely over your set foot. There are limited holds, so be ready to place a foot on the same hold your hand still occupies, or has barely left. Always practice getting rests. One technique that's particularly useful when you're pumped is hooking your hand around a hold, so that you're weighting the section of hand between wrist and pinky. You can use your feet on rock edges to pull your weight close to the wall – even more so on plastic holds. And practice downclimbing, so that you can do it confidently when you hit a puzzling move during a competition. By reversing to your last rest, you can regain strength and psyche, and can take another look.

"When competing, make certain everything is as light as possible: no huge chalk bag, no Clydesdale harness, no figure-8s or locking crabs or widgets hanging off your back. Break in a new pair of shoes for competition by climbing in them for about three weeks. Set them aside before they get much more worn.

"The night before an event, pack all your gear. Chalk bag (with stout loops! Hugo Alvarado lost his at Snowbird – it ripped off and sailed away), chalk bag string, shoes, jacket or sweatshirt, and outer pants if you want them. I pack a little bottle of rubbing alcohol and a toothbrush to clean my shoes just before I go out. Take an extra pair of socks to wear over your shoes as you walk out to the wall.

"Walkman? Check. Tapes? Check. It's great when they let you climb to your own music, but I've twice now gone to the pleasant trouble of picking out tunes, then – curses! – forgotten my Perry Como cassette.

"Optional . . . needle and thread, maybe a small pair of scissors. They come in handy for all kinds of things. Also, a book or magazine or pen and paper – you could be waiting a good long time for your turn on the wall. Recently, Will Gadd of Canada drew to climb last – and waited 10 hours! Depending on the venue, you may or may not be served food while (if) you wait. I always bring a small water bottle and some food. For me, that's a chocolate shake and a chili dog (OK, joke - a banana and a Power Bar). Go with what you usually do. You're best off with fruit and complex carbs before the event.

"Even if you're staying in a hotel, consider bringing your own food for breakfast. Again, you don't want to deviate much from what you usually have. I bring cereal and some dried milk.

"OK. You've eaten breakfast, arrived and signed in. Backstage, in 'isloation,' everyone's languishing around. I quite like this part, lying around, talking. Every competition should have a practice wall or area, or at least some gym equipment. Most climbers prefer to get a good pump, maintain it for about ten minutes, then loose it about an hour prior to competing, but it's hard to manage that as you don't know exactly when you'll climb. All you can do is estimate, based on the time limit per competitor, and recalculating as

contestants come and go. Also, beware of getting caught in the cold. People sometimes are called onto the rug when they'd thought they still had an hour to wait.

"Each person's pre-climb ritual is as individual and personal (and embarrassing) as what we each do in front of the mirror. My custom is not very elaborate (that's pre-climb custom, not my mirror capers, which are none of your business), and deals mostly with audio-visuals. I remember great and inspired climbing performances I've seen, and certain comments I've heard. I hear Jim McCarthy saying, as he watched Scott Franklin smoothly pulling up on one hold after another at the first Snowbird World Cup, 'Scotty's climbing well,' or England's Martin Atkinson, at the World Cup in Leeds, England, saying as Robyn Ebersfield cruised up the wall, 'Got a cool head for competitions, doesn't she?' I remember a line from a Life Magazine story about the climbing world's top female dog, Lynn Hill. Referring to an upcoming event, she said, 'When I go out there, everything will be crystal clear.' In my mind I see that line on the white page, even the kind of type used.

"Well – time to go out. Not to tempt fate, but . . . if anything unseemly happens, like you trip or stumble, or walk past the wall, put it straight out of your mind. You need to be humorous and no-nonsense with yourself, particularly on the wall. In Berkeley this year, I had an awful slip and was very lucky to catch myself on the fly. 'Don't even *think* about it,' I mock-scolded. Ten feet later, I did fall off, and only as I was lowering did I remember the slip.

"Overall, I think the biggest mistake inexperienced people make is not *looking around* enough. Plan, plan, plan, starting during the time period (usually two minutes) you're given to inspect the wall. Look at the moves absolutely as hard and far as you can, imagining probable sequences. Look around corners and arêtes and above roofs and memorize where holds are. You may want to pick out a corresponding notch, rivet, or hold – something – on the near or under side of a feature, in case once you're underway you can't lean out to spot holds. I learned the hard way to look over the quickdraws all the way up the route. At Leeds, I got under a roof, leaned out and peered over the lip only to see no holds. I finally spotted a quickdraw about eight feet out right. By the time I saw it, I'd lost some strength. The point is, I hadn't traced the route's whole line via the quickdraws.

"On the ground, however, I was looking hard at the wall but couldn't see how to do the first crux, through the first little roof. The timer told me my time had started, but I thought, 'I can't go, I don't see how to do this.' I made myself stand still till suddenly, I saw the sequence. The move took down several people, but I was OK because I could go quickly and avoid getting pumped. The point came home again when I was watching Didier Raboutou on the superfinal. He spent long moments beyond his allotted viewing time mostly scrutinizing a funky low move. It was worth it.

"Be optimistic, and just concentrate on the moves. Don't think about where so-and-so might have gotten to, or what place you hope to get. Just get up there and do the job.

"As you begin, remember to breathe. Look for rests. And let yourself enjoy the climbing. The more you like the route and the holds, the better you'll do.

"When you need to be dynamic, think in terms of power glides rather than lunges. If you must lunge, commit to it all out, and remember to *grab*.

"When you come to a hard part, don't be tempted to thrash on through. Hang on. Figure it out. But when you *have* to go for it, go fast. For example, if you reach a hold above a roof, swoop those feet right up.

"Look several moves ahead. You may not have time to tinker on a roof; holds can go from decent to time-bomb so fast. If you don't see from below that you have to get a hold with a certain hand, you may realize it too late.

"Forget the crowd, seductive as its presence and voices are. It can make you feel as if you're doing better than you are, and can goad you on too soon. At Leeds, Catherine Destivelle stepped up and down three times at one ugly little roof before making a try and popping off. Afterwards, she said she had let herself be swayed by the shouts of 'Allez!' and 'Go for it!' from below. 'I hear ze crowd and I am . . . entranced,' she said, chuckling. 'And so I go, even though I am not all right in my mind for ze move. In ze future, I must listen only to myself.'

"OK, you've hit trouble, and your demise is nigh. Never just give up – when you think you can hang on no longer, you probably can eke out *one* more move – and *never* grab the rope (horrors!). 'At least die trying,' as John Long (rogue that he is) wrote in "The Only Blasphemy." You might latch that hold after all. And then another, and another, and isn't that what it's all about?"

An exemplary treatise, granted. But Ms. Osius leaves one question unanswered: What does our darling do in front of her mirror?! She says just a little 'air-climbing' (a climber's version of shadow-boxing), but she's too tall and too smart to be believed here.

The mighty Lynn Hill (five-foot zero, 101 lbs.) is arguably the most famous rock climber in the world. She deserves to be. On a competive circuit clogged with Europeans, Lynn is the world champion, and continues to dominate. Moreover, her adventure climbing exploits are no less distinguished – harrowing El Cap peg-ups, first free ascents of wilderness walls – she's done it all; and always with such power, grace and style that even her staunchest rivals applaud her success. She is a true champion. Let's conclude our business with the physical aspects of climbing by listening to Lynn's views on competitions, knowing her insights will serve us on all genres of climbing.

"Good or bad, competition is a quality inherent in human nature. It has been, and most likely will continue to be, a factor in human evolution.

"Competition was a driving force in climbing long before the first organized meets took place. Climbers the world over always have strived to climb faster, higher, in better style, without bottled oxygen, etc. In so doing, climbers have competed against one other, against the rock or mountain, and always against themselves.

"Initially, organized competitions stirred a great controversy among many top European and American climbers; for various reasons, many of these climbers boycotted the first competition, held in Bardonecchia, Italy, in 1985. Once climbers understood that competitive climbing was a separate game that neither infringed or demeaned climbing on natural rock – and that there was money to be made – most hold-outs chose to compete in the second annual Sport Rocchia competition, also held in Italy, in 1986. This was my first experience in a free-climbing competition.

"This 1986 competition showed how hard it was to organize and structure a fair and consistent venue to measure performance. It could hardly be otherwise for a new sport, and I was not surprised that the rules and format were vague and poorly thought out. I was completely shocked, however, when the meet organizers changed the rules to enable a well-known European climber to win!

"There were other disturbing aspects of this competition as well. The match was held on a cliff some ways off the road, and hundreds of spectators completely ravaged the verdant hillside getting there. From the base, the viewing was excellent – because all the trees had been chopped down! The rock was trashed as well: holds were chipped, pockets were plugged up with cement, all to create routes of the desired difficulty.

"Though they should have been the primary impetus, enviormental considerations did not spur on the development of artificial walls specifically designed for competitions. Rather, bad weather, convenience of location (for spectators and the media), and the ease of fashioning fair and perfectly-tailored routes quickly made artificial walls the prefered medium for virtually all competitions.

"Despite the refinements in design, artificial walls are by no means a perfect simulation of natural rock, nor is climbing in a competition comparable to climbing with friends at a favorite crag. Competitions and artificial walls are simply another facet of climbing, one that provides a new form of play, fresh

Lynn makes good use of the available holds at the World Cup in Berkeley, California.

Beth Wald photo

Lynn Hill demonstrates flexability at a compettition at Nimes, France.

Beth Wald photo

challenges and a novel kind of learning experience. As a result of competing, I have learned much about myself with respect to the psychological elements of the game, while my actual climbing prowess has steadily improved.

"Since all actions are directed by the nervous system, either by conditioned responses or automatic reflexes, the brain is key in determining one's physiological potential. Genetics, natural ability, physical training and experience, also are critical factors in reaching one's potential. Yet one's attitude is no less vital to success – that conscious element that we are free to cultivate and improve through a better understanding of ourselves.

"There are many talented climbers capable of winning on a given day. Most have the necessary strength, technique and experience to win. What generally prevents a person from optimum performance are mental distractions, or mental blocks. Through my own experiences, and observation of others in many competitions, I have identified a whole range of mental errors. High anxiety is the most common; it usually stems from a lack of confidence or a fear of failure. This most likely expresses itself when full concentration and confidence are needed most. A momentary mental distraction during a crux move has sent more than one anxious competitor off the wall. Anxiety simply wastes strength. You tense up, overgrip handholds, and climb stiff and awkwardly. Your thinking becomes limited and rushed, and often you commit to a hastily-planned sequence. You also can create excess anxiety by placing too much importance on winning. This attitude inhibits your ability to relax and directs your thinking contrary to what you'll need to perform optimally. Generally, you'll perform best when you have a true desire to climb for the inherent pleasure it brings.

"We all have off days, when the desire and spark simply are not there. If an off day coincides with a competition, more effort is needed to redirect one's state of mind. In such cases, I try to reinforce positive performance qualties and review certain mental affirmations. I imagine how I would like to perform, rather than on how I'd like to feel. Override negative thoughts and feelings by feeding yourself positive performance goals. Since my best climbing experiences occur when I have an intense desire to climb, I overcome ennui by recreating this state of mind. Before competing, I recall positive climbing experiences, remembering as vividly as I can how I felt on those special days, thereby reinforcing a similar level of concentration, sense of rhythm and enthusiasm.

"During the warmup period, I concentrate on moving in a relaxed fashion, without exerting any more energy than necessary. Just before climbing, I close my eyes and enter a progressive relaxation ritual, scanning my body for any sensation of tension. If I find any tense spots, I focus on releasing that tension. I also cultivate a sense of well being, while reaffirming my intention to climb focused and relaxed. In the isolation area, it's usually possible to hear clapping and shouting from the audience. This can greatly magnify one's level of excitment and anxiety, particularly if the person climbing before you is performing well. But after dozens of competitions, I've learned to deal with these pressures. Although competition measures the ability of each person relative to the others, it should not be considered a 'battle' between contestants, or even a fight against the wall. The people I compete 'against' are a community of friends and peers with whom I share my passion for climbing.

"Rather than charging the wall like a gladiator, I direct my thinking in a way that allows me to be clear and confident. I maintain a balance between my level of excitement and relaxation. Whether I am climbing at a competition or at a crag, I can shine only if I reach this state. Only then can I react intuitively, creating a sort of harmony between my actions and what the climb requires. As soon as it becomes a battle, I tense up, can no longer react naturally, and the harmony is lost.

"The trick is to realize the qualitative difference between 'fighting,' and focusing my efforts and desire to respond to the best of my ability.

"My actual competition strategy is simple: At the wall, I take enough time to look around, to percieve all possible holds and devise the probable sequence. Once I decide on a sequence, I commit 100% of my focus and effort to it, no matter how desperate it seems.

"On days when everything flows together, I reach a state of pure concentration that allows me to be keenly perceptive and to react spontaneously. These are the experiences I seek, whether I am in a competition or simply climbing for myself."

We could spend 50 pages examining the physical aspects of competition climbing and never exhaust the topic. On the other hand, Christian Griffith, a member of America's first climbing team, thinks an appropriate mental outlook is the most important factor. Says Christian:

"I have heard many competitors tell me about their 'positive attitude' before a big meet. Many of these climbers fall in the first 15 feet. Competitions are mentally taxing, so never mind the sham 'positive attitude,' which is most times a means to rationalize failure. A good competitive showing is a great experience, and a poor one is mortifying; don't waste time and energy thinking about either before the event. Enter the competition with a blank mind, and your body will perform to the best of its experience and training. It's this vacant, 'silent observer' state that has seen me through my best ascents. The degree to which I can attain this state determines my success in competitions."

RAW SPEED

I can't leave off competitions without reviewing what is quickly becoming the show-stopper of every venue that features it: speed climbing.

First seen in Eastern European countries (particularly in the Soviet Union), speed climbing has become an increasingly important part of most American competitions, depending on the size and timetable of the meet. In most competitions, a lack of time means organizers are hard-pressed to get all the contestants up the wall. But if time and facilities allow, a special speed-climbing event will generate a lot of interest and rave reviews. From a spectator's point of view, speed climbing is far more exciting than the technical event.

The courses usually are set up to allow rapid passage, featuring long and wild dynamic climbing between jug holds. Get a mad-dog speed climber chomping at the bit, goaded on by a couple hundred pushy spectators and the joker on the

mike, and watch out! The 100-yard dash has got nothing over this event.

For those interested in speed climbing, let's cue up Hans Florine, who routinely takes the gold at speed-climbing events:

"I imagine I am throwing the holds to the ground. Generally, you can do two short moves faster than one long dyno, which saps strength for the following moves. Forget the methods of conventional 'difficulty' climbing, where you grab a hold, reposition your hand on it, milk it, huff off it, crimp on it, chalk off it, and finally crank off it. Almost all competition speed routes are 'jug hauls,' so work the holds with that in mind. Usually, you're allowed to watch other competitors climb the route; take advantage of that opportunity and study their moves. I've filched at least two moves at every competition by watching other speed climbers at work, and this had given me faster times on the wall. If you're allowed to rehearse the route prior to the competition, try to work out a good sequence for the last 10 to 15 feet, because that's where you are apt to be pumped and stupid. There usually is a bell or buzzer on the top of the wall, so never fail to hit it!!"

Rock Games

CHAPTER 9

FREE SOLOING

If a climber wants to risk his life, that's his decision, but to encourage anyone to solo is to reserve a place in hell. Consequently, talking about free soloing makes me a little edgy. It also makes my palms sweat. I've soloed just enough to know both the beauty and the horrors of the venture, and am leery of over- or understating either side.

Scrambling unroped over easy terrain is a required part of climbing. 'Third classing' routes approaching your technical limit is not. Yet climbers do solo, and will continue to solo. So to ignore the topic altogether, to withhold information that possibly could save a person's life, seems recklessly mean and narrow-minded. Instead, I will pass on all that I can, hoping to limit the genuine risks.

No one argues that soloing is climbing in its purest form. That so few soloists fall suggests that sober, calculated judgement prevails over the naive notion of the foolish daredevil going off half-cocked. Herman Buhl, Reinhold Messner, Royal Robbins, and more recently, John Bachar and Peter Croft – some of the true legends of our sport – all have reputations fashioned, in part, from soloing. Still, while we laud these climbers, a definite taboo shrouds their exploits. Certainly, difficult soloing is reserved for the full-blown expert, for those who eat, sleep, and drink climbing. But even for accomplished soloists the practice is a mine field full of clear and subtle dangers.

The likelihood is much overstated, but one should never get lured into soloing through peer pressure or dubious ambitions, like achieving fame. It's undeniable that many active climbers routinely solo easy, or even moderate, routes. A very few solo desperate routes (5.11 and up). But I've also known plenty of world-class climbers who never solo, no matter how easy the terrain – and if anything, their reputations have grown from their forbearance. The point is, soloing is one aspect of the sport where you cannot, or should not, emulate other climbers (save for those who never solo).

What then, is the lure? By dint of the frank jeopardy involved, soloing evokes feelings of mastery and command, plus a raw intensity that even a million-dollar-a-year ball player will never experience – not in the Super Bowl, not in the World Series, not on center court at Wimbledon. And therein lies the snare. Following a particularly rewarding solo, when everything has clicked, the climber feels like a magician. These very feelings can actually foster a sham sense of invincibility. Hence, it's not unheard of that a narrow escape is followed by an eagerness to push things just a tiny bit further, and so on, until the soloist is courting doom. And he'll most assuredly find it if he doesn't quickly back off. The whole insidious business is closely tied to anything that is exhilarating, deadly and fiendishly addictive. Whenever desire overrides judgement, bad things happen. If the soloing fool is fortunate, he'll have a harrowing close call, and he won't be the first to swear, 'Never again!'

Conversely, soloing has provided me with some of the sharpest, and greatest, experiences of my climbing career. Particularly on longer routes, the charged mix of fear and focus strips away any masks, exposing the most fundamental self. It's one way of finding out, once and for all, who you really are. It's also a sure way to die if so much as a single toehold pops. Understand this: The potential penalties simply are too high to rationalize risking your life to scale a section of stone. Wrap your reasoning in rarified language, and maybe you'll touch on a vague truth. It's also true that my friend Tobin Sorrenson – a talented, beautiful and outrageous young man – died while soloing the North Face of Mount Alberta. His death, at age 24, showed me the unforgiving side of the game, minus all the poetry and shimmering sunsets. It was a personal revelation of another, perhaps more significant kind. You just want to slog home and hug your child, kiss your wife, call your mom – tell someone you care about how much you love them. And if they want to go soloing, you don't ignore them. You pass on everything you can that might help their singular odyssey.

I defer here to John Bachar, who throughout his remarkable career has continually redefined the possible, both with his unprecedented solos and his revolutionary roped ascents. Anyone even remotely interested in soloing would do well to memorize what follows. This is excerpted from Bachar's *Quick Guide to Free Soloing:*

It's not the fall that kills you. It's the landing.

– Pete Moss

"Free soloing is a profound and far-reaching contest of the climber with himself. The game can grant remarkable feelings of freedom – and quite possibly the most exhilarating moments of your life. Just the same, my purpose here is neither to encourage or dissuade you from free soloing, rather to furnish helpful suggestions to those few who desire to try this beautiful style of climbing. First, an overview.

"Free soloing must be approached sanely and soberly, and it's vital to have a firm grasp of both the risks a soloist will face, and the precautions he should take. We must accept the fact that, at best, free soloing is calculated risk. Apart from our apparent subjective control of the situation, there always exist objective hazards, totally outside our control, that may cause us to fall. An astute appraisal of the circumstances – *before* the solo – can help limit these

(opposite)
Peter Croft solos the *"Bearded Cabbage,"* Joshua Tree

Bob Gaines photo

objective risks. Several rules are obvious:
- Choose routes that don't have loose rock.
- Don't climb below other parties.
- Watch for cascading rappel ropes.

"Other objective risks are harder to reduce and even harder to anticipate. Ever had a bat wing out of a crack and into your face while you were climbing? Or how about a wasp attack, or a gut ache? Don't even think about an earthquake. The list goes on. After we have minimized potential objective hazards as much as possible, we must accept the fact that we can still die as a result of outside influences. We must always remain aware of this, but never let the thought affect our concentration.

"That much accepted, we confront the subjective dangers. Basically, there is but one: To make a gymnastic error that could result in a fall. We insist that a free soloer is an expert, so gymnastic errors and faulty technique are caused by poor concentration and judgement rather than a lack of technique. To help develop bullet-proof concentration, begin soloing routes that gymnastically are very easy for you. This helps promote the needed relaxation to climb with a minimum of lost motion and wasted energy. The moment concentration and calm wane, muscles tense, technique suffers and the odds quickly mount against the soloist. When you're soloing properly, it feels like you're right above the ground. You're aware only of the moves before you and of the pleasure of moving effortlessly up the stone. If you're preoccupied with falling, your concentration suffers and you certainly don't belong up there. Ponder this: What is the difference between doing a 5.1 move a foot off the ground and doing one a thousand feet up? Physically, there is no difference. Once the soloist has a firm grasp of this concept he is free to try and master it. Once mastered, he most likely can solo wherever his technique is superior to that needed to scale a given route.

"**Some thoughts on starting out:** Free soloing should only be attempted by experienced and dedicated climbers who are in excellent climbing shape. These three things – experience, dedication and superb fitness – are requisite to foster the truly key ingredient – confidence. Initially, choose routes that are well below your technical limit (several grades, at least). Say you can climb 5.11 on a toprope and can lead most 5.10s. Start with a short, classic 5.5 or 5.6 route that you're very familiar with and that you have absolutely no doubt about being able to climb without falling off. On that initial solo, the first battle any sane person will have will be with their own mind. Go with a simple, straightforward solo the first time out, and keep that battle lop-sided in your favor.

"**Some thoughts on downclimbing:** The ability to downclimb is the soloist's strongest protection system. Practice downclimbing from the outset. The soloist should always feel confident that he can downclimb anything he goes up. The continual awareness of one's capacity to reverse moves as one performs them is the best way of gauging whether or not one is attempting a route that is too difficult. As a rule, solo only those routes that you can downclimb.

"The soloist must have both great downclimbing technique and the capacity to memorize and reverse complex sequences of moves. The best way to develop these techniques is to practice on boulders. Learn to downclimb every boulder problem you can, gaining valuable confidence on crux-like moves without the penalty of a grievous fall. Once you have practiced on the boulders, you can begin practicing on actual routes. Climb up 10 feet, then downclimb. Later, climb up 20 feet and downclimb. Once you can downclimb from any position, you can solo with far greater confidence and safety.

"Some thoughts on rehearsed solo – The Solo Circuit: Developing a circuit of routes that you can comfortably solo is the best and safest way to become proficient at the art. The circuit should consist of routes you have done before and are very familiar with. Start the circuit with easy warm-up solos and move on to harder solos only if you are climbing well. That first circuit should be a modest one; augment the circuit slowly and cautiously.

"Soloing is not a casual enterprise, and the soloist is best advised to stay sharp at his craft. To solo safely and confidently, you must solo at least a couple times a week, mixing it in with your other climbing activities. Once you have established a solo circuit of a dozen or so routes, you'll be surprised at the amount of climbing you can do in a very short time. This helps maintain your soloing edge and your gymnastic flow up the stone.

"A word of caution: Never solo when you are tired or have low energy. One of the temptations on a solo circuit is to keep soloing even when fatigued. Knowing you have soloed the entire circuit dozens of times, and yearning that last blast of adrenaline is often sufficient to lure you into the danger zone, when your technique is sloppy and concentration wanting. The good soloist is in touch with his body – as is any good athlete. He knows when he is tired, and above all, he knows when to stop.

"Some words on on-sight soloing: Once a soloist has served an apprenticeship on rehearsed solos, he may choose to attempt an on-sight solo of an established route. Clearly understand that this is an entirely different game than rehearsed soloing. If the on-sight solo is a hard one, the soloist must be nothing less than a brilliant on-sight leader, for his ability to flawlessly visualize and execute successive sequences is truly a matter of life and death. He also must be able to predetermine his ability to downclimb the visualize sequence; again, the ability to downclimb is absolutely crucial during on-sight solos. It's your only protection system. Always be prepared to back off, and never attempt moves you are not certain you can reverse if need be. Ironically, it often is difficult to admit to ourselves that a solo simply is too difficult just then, and to do the wise thing and downclimb off. Soloing accidents most often occur when climbers foolishly push on in poor form. You can fool other climbers about how solid, or marginal, you were, but never try and fool yourself. Back off it if it doesn't feel perfect.

"Some thoughts on soloing a face versus a crack: Soloing cracks is generally more secure than soloing face climbs. Cracks normally offer far more surface contact with the rock, and faulty footwork rarely causes the disastrous results it does on face climbs. But much depends on the manner of face we are soloing. Minor foot slippage may or may not be so devastating if we are soloing up buckets. On slab and edging routes, however, perfect footwork is crucial.

"Slab and friction routes are far and away the most treacherous to solo. Surface contact is minimal, and the smallest mistake can send you off. You'd better be a full-blown slab guru to even consider soloing a hard one. They require utmost precision in the footwork department.

"Steep face commonly is more secure than slabs, though less secure than cracks. Much more emphasis is placed on the upper body, especially the fingers and forearms, on steep faces. To feel comfortable soloing steep faces, the soloist must have ample reserves in the forearms. And you never want to get so pumped that you cannot downclimb to safety.

"Some mental considerations: The feelings of exhilaration, freedom and control that come from soloing are very powerful. And very tempting. The soloist is ever tantalized to try something just a little more challenging each time he solos. The wise soloist is he who has the same control over his desire as he has over his climbing technique. As the saying goes, 'He who knows that enough is enough, will always have enough.'

"Some of the worst moments of my life have come after feeling out of control on a free solo. The most important ambition is not attaining the summit, but rather achieving that extraordinary state of control over mind, body and gymnastic movement, all while staring your own death right in the eyes. This state of fluid motion, piercing concentration and unshakable control is the real goal of the art of free soloing."

Calculation. Precisely knowing his limit. That's John's game. And don't forget that every one of John's solos are backed up by nearly 20 years of climbing experience, and most of those years were spent climbing at a top grade. In short, he knows exactly what he's doing. If you don't, and still want to go soloing, call up your loved ones for a final chat, enjoy a fine meal, pray the Rosary, then huff down a last smoke and get set to meet your maker. And when you're at the base, gazing up at the rock, review the soloist's code: "If there is any doubt about it, forget it!" If you do cast off, make certain you're doing so for your own good reasons.

NEW ROUTES

To establish a new route is to make a timeless statement. While many climbers like the timeless part – knowing their name will live on in guidebooks – an equal number forget the statement bit. Making a bad statement, thus a bad route, is to invite eternal infamy. So it's essential to do things right the first-time around, particularly if bolts are to be placed. I won't encourage or instruct climbers to establish new routes. Better to recall an incident that happened some years ago in the cafeteria at Yosemite.

I was with a Canadian climber who was then recognized as a master wall climber. Only 24, he'd already put up several new routes on El Capitan. A younger climber came to our table and asked my friend for advice about bagging big new walls. My friend suggested that our visitor go to some scrappy area where nobody ever climbed and experiment on short routes first. After he felt comfortable on one-pitch routes, perhaps then the young man could move on to bigger routes. Our guest, who already had a catalog of big walls to his credit, scorned this advice. After all, he noted, the first new climb my friend ever bagged was a grade 6 whopper on El Capitan. "True," my friend stated, "but I didn't have to ask anyone how to do it."

Take a lesson from this. Make damn certain you know what you're doing before you start drilling, or you'll live to regret it. While nobody really can tell you how to go about establishing new routes, I can tell you a few things about how not to do it.

First, every sport has something – some procedure, some tangible entity – that is sacred. In boxing, you don't head-butt or hit low. In baseball, you don't touch the ump. In climbing, you don't doctor the rock. Ever. The rock does not belong to you, or even to your generation. Clearing off loose rock and detritus is one thing, but the second you start fashioning the stone for the sake of climbing, you're crossing the line, and deserve whatever scorn is thrown your way.

Darrell Hensel working on a new route at Suicide Rock, California.

Kevin Powell photo

Whenever you have to bolt, regardless of the local ethics, think long and hard about it. If you're blazing a first ascent that requires no drilling, not much can be pinned on you. If the route's a junker, it's the rock's fault. The worst that can be said of you is that you have a poor eye for a line. Once you start drilling, however, you're changing things for all time. Never mind the supposed glory. Is the climb worth it? Is it a good line? What is so special about it that you should drill holes into the rock? The fact that the climbing will be hard is never reason enough to drill holes, because any sparsely-featured piece of rock offers hard climbing.

Always remember that you have to hang your name on whatever you do. If you think the sheer technical difficulty of the route justifies modifying the rock, think about 10 years ahead. Your blockbuster will be yesterday's news. But if it features fine positioning, stimulating climbing, novelty and class, it will be today's classic.

Lastly, always respect local ethics, and never alter an established route. Enough said.

ADVENTURE CLIMBING

It's ironic that the term 'adventure climbing' would ever be coined. Prior to about 1980, virtually all climbing was an adventure. Certainly, a climber could stitch a crack with nuts, or stick with relatively harmless slab routes; but on the main, doubt, committment, jeopardy and a major dose of both fear and exhilaration were the very things that vitalized the game. Hard climbing was as much a matter of confronting your own fears as it was scaling a given cliff.

In one sense, it's sad that short test pieces have come to so dominate the present climbing mentality. The once obligatory credo – that active climbers must tackle the longer routes or they weren't considered 'real' – is now a dated notion. Never mind the macho posturing and pretense in such a credo. The concept was valid enough: The task of climbing a long route not only requires more from the climber (chiefly, a testing of spirit) than merely scraping around short cliffs, however horrendous, but it also offers greater rewards in terms of intensity and lasting memories. Make no mistake about it: Climbers who limit themselves strictly to 'clip-and-go' routes are depriving themselves of much of the very best that climbing has to offer, namely, the 'sporting' aspect.

Take the Chouinard/Herbert route on the North Face of Sentinel, in Yosemite. It's a standard long, hard free route. You're half trashed by the time you hump up the two miles of scree and grassy terraces to the base. The first thousand feet of actual climbing is mainly 5.9 and 5.10, with a touch of 5.11 to keep you honest. Then, the wall suddenly rears. A nasty 5.11+ stemming job ends at a sling belay where you know you're on a Yosemite wall. Then, the leader underclings out a hatchet flake, 2,000 feet of air below his boots, cranks over a roof and pumps up 5.11 ground, making certain not to fall because the pro is sketchy. The belayer's shitting cinder blocks. You'll remember those moments, and will savor them more than the time you cranked a 5.14E move ten feet off the ground with a bolt at your navel.

The term 'sportclimbing,' which first surfaced in the 70s, originally did not mean what it does today. In those days, sportclimbing referred to approaching the traditional climbing game from the orientation of a serious athlete. It did not refer to ignoring age-old rules in search of higher numbers. Regardless, the term sportclimbing really is a misnomer in many respects because so many of the actual 'sporting' aspects have been engineered out of the equation. The generic, everyday usage of 'sport' usually refers to certain physical games; and the very thing that makes these games so interesting is the spontaneity of the endeavor – the running back's 'on-sight' read of the defense, the surfer's quick negotiation of the curl of a terrible Pipeline tube, the Grand Prix cyclist's intuitive glide into a turn at 140 mph. When watching a 'sportclimber' attempt a 50-foot route for the 50th time, clipping a bolt every five feet, more than one observer has wondered where the hell the 'sport' is in such a venture. Actually, most of the clip-and-go routes are not sporting at all, rather they are remarkable examples of a physical discipline.

The mistake that we never want to make is to put absolute precedence on this form of climbing. We do not want to generate the false notion that so-called 'sportclimbing' is the best and only mode. Moreover, we must make certain that sportclimbing, distinct and valid as it is, never encroaches on adventure climbing. Climbers must be mature enough to realize and respect the notion that all climbs are not the same. You don't go up on Black Rose, Middle Cathedral – a longish route with longish runouts – with a bulging bolt kit and start installing new bolts simply because your home crag has bolts every body length. Nor do you start crow-barring the bolts out of a clip-and-go route because you feel it is overprotected. In both cases, vanity and utter disregard results in unsanctionable behavior.

Basically, many climbers who are strictly sportclimbers say that jeopardy is not part of their game. Theirs is about doing hard moves, period. Fine. Just don't try and make this philosophy a mandate for all climbers and all climbs.

As a general rule, the more rules you impose upon yourself, the more you will get out of your climbing. This is even more the case when you take on a climb that – owing to its magnitude, isolation, exposure, etc. – places severe restrictions on your method of ascent. And the route need not have staggering numbers to provide you with some lasting memories. As fun and challenging as clip-and-go routes are, sticking strictly with this medium breeds tedium. Once in a while a climber needs a baptism in fear and exhilaration – needs to venture out where certain things are beyond his immediate control. Get onto something long and wild, where you take things as they come. When you see big name sportclimbers free soloing, speed climbing big walls, or climbing in wilderness areas, they're doing nothing more than what we're suggesting here. When you get a chance, jam out to Zion, or Moab, drive a junker down to Mexico and climb at Trono Blanco, hitch up to the Wind Rivers. You'll never regret it, and will appreciate sportclimbing all the more.

BOULDERING

Bouldering dates back to the very dawn of time, vouchsafed by the brilliant Dr. Theodore Whitehead, professor of biblical hermeneutics at Eaton. While examining the Dead Sea scrolls, Dr. Whitehead discovered a remarkable account concerning Seth, second son of Adam. Said account finds Seth wandering through a fruit orchard when he suddenly spotted a "piebald stag" atop a large stone "terrible and precipitous." With visions of venison chops dancing through his bean, Seth girted his loins, mounted the stone and "scaled ferociously." The stag was gone by the time Seth topped out, "much beleaguered and flumoxed." It was not mentioned how Seth got down from the precipitous stone.

In the ensuing 99 thousand years, bouldering has evolved into a supreme activity of strength and style; and even the finest modern practitioners are still constrained to "scale ferociously." Let's listen to Nancy Pritchard, editor of *Rock and Ice* and a fine boulderer, break down some of the particulars.

"Bouldering is the simplest and purest of climbing pleasures, and is a proven way to perfect technique while giving a peerless all-around workout. Individuality is fostered, tenacity rewarded and, more often than not, both humor and humility are nurtured if not required. You need only shoes, possibly a chalk bag, and a rock – no gear, no partner. There are those few who blur the margin between bouldering and soloing – say, on very high boulders – but as a general rule, traditional bouldering falls are not so severe as to kill or seriously hurt you. Downclimbing, acrobatic jumping, and various forms of spotting can lessen any risks. Ultimately, it's as dangerous as you make it. A good session yields a steady flow of adrenaline, which is welcome on dicey high moves and definitely addictive. Best of all, bouldering is a game of immediate gratification – summiting dozens of rocks in a single session. However if you're off form, you may cry a river for never getting a body length off the deck. Recognized boulder problems tend to be hard, lest they'd be overlooked.

"Practice downclimbing and reversing moves. Lowering off dynos, reversing mantels and wondering where the heck that balancy smear went helps save ankles while developing strength and technique. On longer problems, climbing up, then climbing down helps in working out the sequence. You wire the initial moves, ever going higher before reversing, familiarizing yourself with the sequence. When you are confident of your reservoir of strength and ability, you go for it. However, you can rarely reverse moves on boulder problems near or at your technical limit. It's task enough just to go up.

"Most good boulderers not only are good downclimbers, but great jumpers. If you boulder alone and don't flash every problem (and you won't), you'll eventually pump a hand out, a foot will blow off an edge, or some bungled move or another will cast you off. If you know where you are in relation to both the rock and the ground, you have an elevated chance of landing squarely on both feet. The spinning jump to the best landing spot, and the tuck-and-roll both work for emergency exits.

"Spotting is crucial when a boulderer is cranking upside down (or is locked into any funky, awkward attitude), or the landing is poor. But even then some climbers refuse a spot, or favor only a 'girl' spot. ('Grab me by my hips and gently lower me down.') Fine if you're Mr. Olympia spotting an anorexic sportclimber; but if you're a corn-fed man and your girlfriend weighs 98 lbs, the spot is a sketchy one. The realistic goal of a spot is not to catch the climber, but to simply break the fall and keep the head from smacking solid objects. A shrewd spotter stands facing the rock in a volleyball setter position. When you are working out a hard bouldering problem, you might even hand-check with your spot, your hands gently on the climber's back or rump, ready to ease the inevitable the second it occurs. Two – even three – people spotting is not unheard of if the situation demands.

"A great deal of bouldering is contemplative. Each problem is its own project. You complete one, then start afresh at the base of the next. If you fail, you have as many chances as you choose to try again. You try, fail, then sit, pondering your errors. While your forearms revitalize, you evaluate the sequence, search for obscure edges and holds, and focus your efforts to match the physics of the problem. Then it's back at it.

"About bouldering technique: Practice, practice, practice . . . Bouldering requires different combinations of strength, contemplation and technique for different problems. Sequences often are not obvious; the more you boulder, the better you get at deciphering the correct sequence. Consider your body position relative to the rock, don't hold on too tight, and watch your footwork. The boulders are the best place to work on your lockoffs and mantels. Traversing offers a lot of mileage and short falls. And remember, if you're going to climb a certain rock, make certain you have an idea about how to get down. More than one ace has found herself marooned atop a high boulder, with the only immediate option being to try and reverse the hardest piece of climbing she's ever done. Poor sap . . . .

"Limited commitment, little risk, adrenaline, satisfaction of getting to the top numerous times a day – bouldering is pretty much pure joy. It makes you strong, brave (should

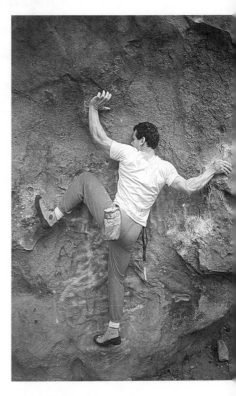

Largo stems it out on the boulders.

Bob Gaines photo

you go for the high ones), hones technique, and gives you good lies for social occasions."

Little need to add much more here. Virtually everyone contributing to this book has stated that bouldering is a prerequisite to arduous climbing. Specialists, who prefer the boulders to the crags, have pushed their art to mind-boggling levels of difficulty – far beyond what is found on the hardest clip-and-go routes.

Good rules to follow are:

• Never climb any higher than where you feel comfortable jumping off from.

• If you must assume an upside down or awkward position, get a spot.

• Remember, if you fall off, you hit the ground. Always clear the ground of the problem stones or any detritus that could cause twisted or broken ankles – the most common bouldering injuries.

• Lastly, strive to develop the boulderer's mentality – that any worthwhile problem takes dozens of tries. Try the impossible. And keep trying. Some day you just might make it. That's what bouldering is all about.

Training

Twenty years ago he was the rare fellow who trained specifically for climbing. Certainly, mountaineers made sure they were 'fit' before heading for the Himalayas, but most rock climbers simply went cragging to get in shape. In many circles, cross-training was considered nonsense. And those who did train often went about things incorrectly. Back then, the focus was on one-arm pull-ups, fingertip chins and a host of other drills that resulted in more injuries than strong climbers. While there is still no definitive work out regime for rock climbers, one thing is for sure: All the finger boards can increase strength, but they also usher in injuries if you do too much cranking on the smaller holds. Also, the whole business about doing millions of pullups a day has been proven to be ineffective. Really, all the specialized workouts have confused, rather than clarified, just what works best. Adding more confusion is the fact that everyone responds differently to different training routines. For this reason, a climber is ultimately left to experiment, and discover what works best for him.

WORKING WITH WEIGHTS

Weight training is an effective way to improve overall body conditioning. The main advantages of a good weight training routine are that you can significantly increase both strength and endurance with no increase in body weight, providing you watch your diet. High strength-to-weight ratio is the aim. A good workout with weights also helps mitigate the fatigue and lack of power that is the bane of most climbers. Climbers who already have technical ability, but lack that last bit of hoist, are best served by such a routine. Others are advised to spend time on the rocks until technique is polished. Once that's accomplished, a cross-training routine is bound to improve performance. Understand that the best strength program cannot make you a heroic climber. At best, strength only can help amplify existing talents.

Any routine you borrow or develop yourself should incorporate certain physiological laws and techniques that often are ignored by climbers, though they are followed religiously by serious weight lifters. The first law is: Train the whole physique, not just the muscles associated with climbing movements. Ignoring muscles with an opposite but complimentary function (antagonistic muscles) produces an imbalanced machine, and makes one injury-prone for a number of reasons. It's fine to emphasize sport-specific muscles, but not at the exclusion of the rest of your body. The second law is: Pick a muscle group, do exercises that best isolate those muscles, and trash them. The third law is: Allow muscles 48 hours to recover before blasting them again.

Ignore any of these precepts and you'll get something less than maximum results. Know that these precepts are not based on any training philosophy or opinion, but rather are based on physiological laws. No one made of flesh and blood can get around them.

THE WORKOUT FROM HELL

To give you an example of a weight training routine that has worked for me, I offer an encapsulated version of The Workout From Hell.

This routine incorporates the conclusive periodization, or 'cycle' program first developed by Russian scientist Matveyev. Matveyev broke training down into four cycles: hypertrophy (size increase), strength, power and peaking. His notion was to phase through this cycle, then follow it with a period of active rest (or important international competition), then repeat the cycle anew. The Workout from Hell simply has taken Matveyev's philosophies and used them to shape a routine tailored to a climber's needs. You'd be wise to incorporate this philosophy as well.

The Workout from Hell involves intense work on specific muscle sets. Basically, I start with 9 to 12 sets (30 reps each) of primary exercises for the arms, back and shoulders. I alternate routines – one day I'll hammer my back and shoulder muscles, the next my shoulders and arms, and on the next, I'll skip the gym, supplementing the weight bit with heavy aerobic conditioning, like jumping rope or bicycling. This goes on for one grueling month.

A note: There are dozens of exercises for each body part. 'Primary' simply refers to the old stand-by 'bomb' motions, which work the muscles most effectively – the basic, fundamental movements. We're talking seated military presses, standing cable or barbell rows and lateral dumbbell raises for the shoulders; preacher E-Z bar curls, seated dumbbell curls, etc. for the guns; close grip presses and flat-back extensions for the triceps. The refining, or finishing, movements – like concentration curls and cable cross-overs – are not part of this routine.

In the next phase of the workout (three weeks), I pile on more weight and cut the reps down to 15. Phase three involves another three weeks of working with even more weight, but only five or six reps per exercise. Phase four is the tapering phase: I do 30, 15 and five reps for each exercise.

Basically, phase one is a conditioning cycle that increases your vascularity and endurance, tones you, conditions your cardio-vascular system and kicks your ass something terrible.

Phase two maintains your endurance and starts working on strength-building commensurate to how much weight you lift.

Phase three goes after raw power, which is summoned

easily after the tremendous conditioning you've gained from the previous two cycles.

The last phase blends everything together.

The second cycle of The Workout From Hell involves the same exercises. Basically, you do 30 reps per exercise during in the first three weeks; 15, 15 and 30 reps during the second three weeks; and 5, 5 and 30 reps, for the third phase. Once again, you're increasing the weight as the reps drop.

The best results will come by focusing on the most fundamental movements, which best blast the muscles. Do not try to incorporate kooky 'climbing' exercises – like massive fingertip pull-ups and one-arm chins – into this routine. Otherwise, you'll be working at cross-purposes. This is the time you should focus on explosive muscular strength, while letting tendons recover and re-knit. And remember, always adhere to a policy of strict form. Try to execute the exercises perfectly; this adherence to form will carry over to your climbing. Form always is more important than the amount of weight you are trying to heft.

Also, be certain to maintain some kind of aerobic, lower body workout – running, cycling, or the king of them all, jumping rope. This is key to your overall conditioning, and keeping your lower body in tune. Moderate lower body weight work also is advisable, if you have the gas to do it.

In addition, you must get adequate rest and east ample cmoplex carbohydrates – spuds and brown rice in particular – to fuel the effort required by a workout of this type.

A word on sports supplements: They vary in quality from pseudo-scientific hogwash to viable products. Still, they are no substitute for eating correctly. And the notion that climbers must load up on excessive protein simply is not true. If you want an energy edge, I would recommend any good carbo fuel/energy drink that supplies complex carbs (from glucose polymers). The good ones will keep you going strong through any workout or climb, however arduous. Anything beyond that is up to you. Read up. And remember, these supplements are secondary to good, balanced grub, high in complex carbs and low in fat.

Largo pumps iron high above the Joshua Tree desert.

Bob Gaines photo

This kind of cycle training gets you remarkably fit, but you must bear two things in mind. First, you cannot keep cranking this type of workout for long – three or four months at the very outside (perfect for the off season). Your body cannot withstand this kind of effort without burning out – or after a while, actually getting weaker. Second, while your base strength increase should stay with you long after you've left the gym, this ultra-peaked form will not last nearly so long. As you start tapering off your routine, you should simultaneously increase your climbing activity, if only slightly. Provided you can make the transition from heavy iron to heavy rock smoothly, your climbing performance should shoot out into the stratosphere for about 20 to 25 days. It is during the last part of this three-week 'peaked' state (that's three weeks after you've left the gym) that you should go for the gold. Try to climb whatever goals you've set for yourself – new routes, 'impossible projects,' whirlwind European tours, Arco championships, et. al.

Most importantly, don't bother with special 'climbing' exercises during this peaked phase. No hang boards or grueling hand traverses. And no weight-lifting at all. Since only a serious climber would ever bother with a routine like the Workout from Hell, such a climber already will have loads of experience and muscle memory at his disposal. When you shift focus from the iron back to the rock, your sport-specific strength – i.e.your cranking power – will skyrocket in a matter of days. Spending grueling hours on hand traverses and hang boards only wastes a limited amount of peaked strength on superfluous activity. Save that strength for ultimate goals. It will be there when you need it, guaranteed.

You will defeat the whole plan if you try to climb at your peak level while performing the Workout from Hell. You don't want to lose your agility, rhythm and chops, however. Two or three short climbing sessions a week at a hard – but not extreme – level should do you. Just maintain your form, and do no more. It's hard to hold back at the crags, but you must if you're after ultimate results.

Lastly, if you really want world-class results, you must live like a world-class athlete. This is something you cannot fake, and there is no denying that traditional notions of fun are given a low priority. It's okay to thread a little pipe, I suppose; but simply lounging around your companion's pad, blowing weed and watching Gomer Pyle reruns just isn't going to get it. Nor is skipping workouts to make another party. You must get adequate rest, and spend some time each day alone, relaxing. Discipline is the name of the game. Many people who have God-given ability simply can't make the sacrifices needed to reach their potential. That's why there's so few world-class climbers out there. The question is: How bad do you want to be one?

The Workout form Hell is just one example of a serious routine. But how about something for those who have neither the time nor the desire for such a program. There are other options. But first understand several principals previously mentioned: 1) You will always most benefit by doing exercises which best isolate a particular muscle, or muscle group; 2) Once you push a muscle to exhaustion, you need at least 48 hours for that muscle to recover. Hence, if you do, say, pull-ups every day, you will get far less from the exercise if you did them every third day, until you dropped.

WEEK-END WARRIOR WORKOUT

Endless different routines are possible. The trick is how to schedule them—that is, when will you work out? There are now many sources from which a climber can learn and devise just what routine he or she will do (pull-ups, hang board work, hand traversing, rope climbing, etc...). The problem is: If you climb on week-ends, it usually takes a day or two to recover, then it's already Wednesday. One, and probably the best schedule, is to workout Monday and Thursday – Monday as hard as you can, and Thursday moderately hard. It's hard to get up for a grueling workout after you've climbed yourself down to the quick the previously two days, but the Monday/Thursday schedule is probably the best for overall results, leaving you sharp for the following Saturday.

The other option, and a favorite for those who disdain regular gym work, is to go bouldering (on indoor climbing) on Wednesday. This keeps you sharp, is a tremendous workout, and gives you two days rest following both the weekends toils, and your mid-week efforts. In the seventies, many of the hardest routes going up were accomplished by climbers following this very schedule: Climb on Saturday and Sunday, back to work on Monday, sneak off on Wednesday for an hour's late afternoon bouldering, then back at it on the weekend.

CIRCUIT TRAINING

The notion here is not to push yourself to muscular exhaustion, but to simply get some exercise. Therefore it is possible to train a little each day, if you feel up to it. Precisely what your circuit will consist of is your call. Most comprehensive circuits involve various stations that give you a good, overall pump, consisting on the whole of free-hand, or calisthenic-type movements – push-ups, sit-ups, dips, etc. . . . This type of training is not particularly effective in building strength or power, but is excellent for overall conditioning. Remember that for optimum results, you should try and get your heartbeat over 120 beats per minute, and keep it there for at least 20 minutes.

FIVE-MINUTE WORKOUT

There is no such thing, really. But you can build an artificial wall, put a pull-up ledge above the wet-bar, tack two artificial holds onto the drywall, and spend five minutes every day toying around, hanging on till you melt off, till you scream. You might not improve your climbing, but it's a good psychological boost just to keep your hand in and your fingers loose.

As the technical envelope is pushed further, debilitating injuries become more commonplace. Aside from the normal muscle tweaks and strains inherent in all sports, climbers particularly are prone to elbow and finger injuries, most of which involve some form of tendonitis. Having suffered these impairments on several occasions, I can assure you that ignoring the injury can result in pain so intense that straightening the arm, or closing the fingers, is virtually impossible – and climbing is out of the question. Concerning treatment for these conditions, I defer to climber/orthopedist Dr. Mark Robinson, who has conducted several studies involving climbing injuries. Writes Dr. Robinson:

"Do the following to self-cure tendonitis:
- Decrease activity until the pain is gone, and all swelling and tenderness disappear.
- Wait two weeks more.
- Start back with easy strength exercises – putty, gum, rubber squeezers – for two to three weeks.
- Do low-angle, big-hold climbing for one month.
- Move to high-angle big-hold climbing for one month.
- Get back to full bore.

"Anti-inflammatory medicines (aspirin, Motrin, Nuprin, Naprosyn, etc.) can be used to control symptoms and speed the recovery process. They should not be used to suppress pain to allow even more use, since this eventually will lead to more problems and a longer recovery period.

"Various mystical and pseudo-scientific remedies, such as dietary modifications, herbal cataplasms, spinal manipulations, electrical machines with imposing control panels, horse liniments, ethnic balms, etc., are at best unproven. Very few, if any of them, bear any conceivable relation to what is known to be the basis of the problem."

What the doctor is telling us is that time and patience are the key ingredients to full recovery, and that returning prematurely to high-stress climbing is as foolish as ignoring the injury in the first place. "The tissues of the musculo-skeletal system are capable of remarkable feats of repair and restoration," Dr. Robinson assures us, "but these processes are slow." Furthermore, there is absolutely no proof that anything in legitimate medicine can accelerate these processes, save the use of anti-inflammatory drugs, which simply eliminate the restrictions and allow the natural healing to proceed. Again, all the fancy gadgets and expensive therapy don't really accomplish a damn thing for tendon injuries. Understand that if you have good insurance, you probably will be referred to a sports medicine clinic. Such establishments are not in business to refuse your money. I've gone through the whole routine at a famous clinic, and after several months was no better off than if I'd simply bought a bottle of generic ibuprofen (Motrin), and spent two months in the library reading Punch. In extreme or very specific cases, an injection of time-release cortisone can work wonders. But it can also do more damage than good. Each injury is a little different, and there is no generic verdict on the long-term effectiveness of cortisone. My father, a surgeon, told me that whenever you try to rush nature, you invariably run into problems. The safest bet is to go the conservative route, and simply wait out the injury.

Injury Prevention

We know the medical experts have told us that certain exercises virtually assure injuries, and that we should avoid these if we're in for the long haul. But aside from that, what can we do? Some support of critical tendons can be achieved by taping. Trouble spots: around the fingers on either side of the main (second) joint; around the wrist; and around the forearm, just shy of the elbow. But professional athletes are relying more and more on two things to avoid injuries: stretching and warming up. Aerobics and yoga might not make you stronger, but they may keep you from getting injured. And a very important practice is to do a little stretching and some easy climbing before jumping onto the main event. Warming up is part of any sport, and should be essential for climbers, whose movements so stress the elbows and fingers. This is particularly true for bouldering. Get limbered up and try and crack a light sweat, then max yourself. And if you tweak something, stop before you make it worse.

This warm-up ritual is vital for those returning from an injury, or nursing a chronic problem. For instance, I have always loved dynamic bouldering, but years of wrenching latches have left me with small bone chips in my left elbow. Specialists have said orthoscopic surgery might help things, but have advised me to just deal with the stiffness until the problem becomes unbearable. If I warm up, the pain usually subsides. If not, it's tortuous.

NUTRITION

The subject of nutrition is so involved and specialized that a climber should approach the topic as a separate study. Much of the best information is published in body-building magazines (also a good source for training tips). Never mind the leviathans; the science of nutrition is well-covered in these magazines. A few trips to the library can help round out your program. In short, we've not the pages to devote to more than a passing look at the subject.

During the Yosemite hay days (the 1970s), climbers ate whatever they could get their hands on. Many climbers still do. But a growing number literally are starving themselves to achieve what they believe will be a greater strength to weight ratio. There are several dangers and misconceptions here. The first misconception is that the lighter you are, the better your strength to weight ratio. This is not categorically true. Several years ago I spent the summer trudging across Borneo. Immediately afterwards, I went to Japan and did some climbing – or tried to. I was rail-thin, but I couldn't climb for shit. No power. I spent the next week bouldering, running, lifting weights and eating prodigious quantities of sushi, plus gallons of saki. Soon, I was back at it. The fact is, everyone has a natural body weight. It's part of your genetic make-up. You can cheat it briefly by reducing calories and eliminating fats altogether; but it's a fact that once you go below 6 percent body fat, it's a game of diminishing returns. Also, trying to keep yourself that lean year round, is an inferior and downright stupid training philosophy.

Eric Johnson balancing physical and mental muscle during a clip-in.

Greg Epperson photo

We have gone into the notion of peaking for brief periods of time to obtain maximum performance. The key here is 'brief.' If you look at any other sport, you'll see that no athlete tries to maintain either top form or 'fighting' weight the year round. Not only is it impossible, it's counter-productive. Your performance should go in phases and cycles, and your weight should as well. That's not to say you should follow a good showing at Snowbird with a six-month binge of Dr. Pepper and Mars bars. The best athletes maintain good fitness and diet year round. But they're experienced and smart enough to realize that both physically and mentally, you've got to give your body a break at least half the time.

Recognize the difference between being in good overall shape, and being absolutely peaked. Good fitness actually makes you less injury prone. But when you're peaked, you're working at the extreme edge of your physical capabilities, and it becomes increasingly possible to overextend yourself; if anything, your body is so highly tuned that it is fragile, in a sense. There are loads of scientific explanations as to why the highly-tuned race car will break down faster than the family wagon. It's also known that if you run a race car at top speed for too long, it eventually will blow up. The problem was best described by Whitey Herzog, ex-manager of the St. Louis Cardinals. He was amazed with the conditioning and prowess of 80s ball players. He likewise was concerned with how fragile they were, a problem he ascribed to absurdly strict dieting. The players simply were too highly tuned to last the duration of a 162-game season. Whitey suggested that once a week his players go out and eat a rare steak and a slab of pie to 'get a little juice on the bone.' They did. Injuries tapered off to minor sprains and the Cardinals won the World Series.

So whatever nutritional program you choose, it should correspond to the cycles of your training and climbing. If your climbing has no cycles, no breaks, if you continually try and stay at your maximum (and whippet-thin), you're going against virtually every modern sports philosophy.

Take two climbers of the same ability and fitness. The one with the 'right head' will prove the superior climber every time. He's the one who knows how to program his mind for performance. He may do this through imaging, visualization, self-hypnosis, relaxation techniques and a host of other methods (some fatuous as smoky crystals), all of which long have been used by athletes to gain a mental edge. Particularly with climbing, where fear can paralyze your strength and resolve, a positive mental state is a basic ingredient to success, and it's mandatory for really hard climbing. Even a God-like mind can not conquer physical limitations (no one climbs a wall with no holds, for instance), but an optimum mental state can greatly enhance genuine physical abilities.

The problem is, how do we weed through all the copper bracelets, rhino horns, incense, mantras and nostrums. How do we separate all the superfluity and rubbish from the few viable techniques that actually can help us? The surest way is to go with what has consistently worked best for most climbers.

From a practical standpoint, we need to know what the notions are and how to employ them to positively improve our climbing. Never mind the grad school lingo. We don't need a thesis, rather a guide, a mental recipe – tangible, straightforward and easily understood. And that's what Eric Horst has given us. Eric is a world-class climber who's published a series of excellent articles on the subject of how the mind influences performance. I've asked Eric to boil it all down and serve up the bare jewels. Says Eric:

"The biggest weapon we have in our quest for peak performance is our mind. It controls everything we do. At top levels, a properly-programmed mind is tantamount to success; a poorly-programed one, to failure.

"The muscles of our body need training to increase strength. The same is true for our 'mental muscle.' However, the benefits of mental training are less tangible than, say, lifting weights. It often requires more disipline to maintain a regular schedule of mental workouts.

"Our goals are the mastery of relaxation, centering and visualization. We accomplish this by practicing *specific techniques and rituals,* simply explained in the three tables that follow. But let's first look at relaxation, centering and visualization in fundamental terms, and get a firm grasp of the concepts:

Relaxation

"Here, our principal aim is the reduction of stress and dispensable muscular tension. Superfluous tension results in over-gripped holds, poor balance and a non-fluid, rigid style. Hard moves become harder because improper (non-specific) muscular tension unavoidably pits one muscle against the others.

TABLE 1: THE PROGRESSIVE RELAXATION SEQUENCE

Perform the following procedure at least once a day. At first, it will take about 15 minutes – with practice, much less. Be sure to flex *only* the muscle(s) specified in each step - this is a valuable skill quickly learned. For rapid results, make a tape of these steps (one step per minute), and play it back as you perform the sequence.

1. Go to a quiet room and sit or lie in a comfortable position.
2. Close your eyes, take five deep breaths, and feel yourself 'let go.'
3. Tense the muscles in your lower leg (one leg at a time) for five seconds. Become aware of the feeling, then 'let go,' and relax the muscle completely. Recognize the difference between feeling tense and relaxed.
4. Perform the same sequence with the muscles in the upper leg. Tense for five seconds . . . then relax. Compare the difference.
5. Move to the arms. Start below the elbow, making a tight fist for five seconds, then relax.
6. Tense the muscles of the upper arm (one gun at a time) . . . and relax.
7. Move to the torso. As you get better, try to isolate and tense the chest, shoulder, back, and stomach muscles separately.
8. Finish by tensing the face and neck. Relax them completely, noting the feeling of relaxation in each part.
9. Now, concentrate on relaxing every muscle in your body. Scan from head to toe for any muscles that might still be tense. Maintain this state of total relaxation for at least three minutes.
10. Open your eyes, stretch, and feel refreshed; or begin visualization and imagery work; or go to sleep!

"Optimal efficiency ia accomplished by *relaxing all but the muscles necessary for the given motion.* This accomplished, we greatly increase the cranking might of the 'task muscles.'

"This is an aquired skill. First, we learn 'progressive ralaxation,' a procedure for relaxing the entire body in a matter of minutes (See table). Once that is mastered, we quickly can learn 'differential relaxation,' where we relax all but task-required muscles. With practice, we can accomplish this in the middle of a 5.14 crux. The concept is simple; doing so is not. Practice in the gym. For instance, when doing pull-ups, try relaxing everything but the pulling back and arm muscles, and so on.

"On the rock, experiment with different levels of muscular tension while both moving and resting. Strive to find the minimum level of contraction necessary to stay on the stone. Practice often. You'll soon climb with added grace and less effort. In time, the practice will become automatic.

Centering

"Centering is a simple, yet effective means of gaining and maintaining optimum control of our mind and body as we start a difficult route. When we're centered, we feel strong, confident, relaxed, balanced and keenly aware of our center of gravity.

"Centering requires us to focus our thoughts inward, mentally checking and adjusting our breathing and level of muscular tension. Do this regularly, and you'll learn to conteract any involuntary changes that may have occured due to the pressure of the situation (like hyperventilation, over- gripping, sewing-maching leg, etc.).

"The most effective method of centering is the "Instant Calming (or Centering) Sequence" (ICS). This simple, five-step procedure (see table) provides us with exceptional inner control, even in the face of grim runouts. The ICS is simple to learn and use, especially if you've mastered the aforementioned relaxation techniques. Initially, it will take some minutes to perform; with practice you can get centered in a matter of seconds, or even with a single breath.

"Use the ICS any time you feel rushed, stressed, or scared. Practice at home, or at work – the more you practice, the better and more effectively you can apply the skill to your climbing. Center yourself before every climb, and re-center at every shake-out or rest. This momentary clearing and readjustment will renew your control of mind and body, and enhance your performance on the remainder of the route.

TABLE 2: THE INSTANT CENTERING SEQUENCE (ICS)

The ICS should be performed in an upright position – either sitting or standing. You can perform the sequence almost anytime or anywhere, as long as your eyes are open and you're alert. At first, take a few minutes and slowly go through the steps. With practice, you'll eventually be able to do it in a second or two.

1. Uninterrupted Breathing: Continue your current breathing cycle, concentrating on smooth, deep and even breaths.

2. Positive Face: Flash a smile, no matter your mental state. Research shows that a positive face 'resets' the nervous system so that it's less reactive to negative stress. You'll feel the difference immediately.

3. Balanced Posture: Lift your head up, shoulders broad and loose, back comfortably straight, and abdomen free of tension. A balanced posture makes you feel light, with a sense of no effort in action. A tense and collapsed posture restricts breathing, reduces blood flow, slows reactions, and magnifies negative feelings.

4. Wave of Relaxation: Perform a 'tension check.' Scan all your muscles in a quick sweep to locate unnecessary tension. Let go of those tensions, making your body calm while your mind remains alert.

5. Mental Control: Be focused, positive and uninhibited about the task at hand. Acknowledge reality, and go with the flow!

Visualization

"Proper visualization provides a mental blueprint for our bodies to execute. By creating and repeating this 'mental movie,' mentally watching ourselves flawlessly climb a given section, we program it into our mind as reality, and now have a tangible 'experience,' or guide, showing the way. Correctly visualizing ourselves climbing the crux is truly an invaluable aid, absolutely essential for extreme routes; accordingly, *Visualization is the most important exercise for attaining peak performance.*

"You probably already are performing mental rehearsals of a route you are working on. Proper visualization, however, goes far beyond the easy task of reviewing crux sequences. Try to create detailed 'movies' of touch, sound, and color, along with the kinesthetic 'feel' of actually doing moves. Even imagine the shake-outs and rests, where you will perform the relaxation and centering techniques discussed earlier.

"To learn visualization, imagine youself climbing from an observer's point of view. Watch yourself performing the moves perfectly - smooth and effortlessly - from bottom to top. Imagine clearly even the slightest details, and incorporate positive images of 'flow' and being 'right-on.' Nix any negative and self-defeating images, because these glitches can easily become reality.

"With practice, you'll soon be able to perform internal visualization, where you envision every detail as you would

---

TABLE 3: VISUALIZATION STRATEGIES

1. Practice visualizing and imagining with all your senses. Work on developing your ability to create vivid mental pictures of people, places and events. The more you practice, the better you will get.

2. Imagine your senses in explicit detail. Remember, the more vivid the image, the more powerful the effect.

3. Use photographs, beta sheets, or videotape to improve the accuracy of the mental movies of yourself climbing.

4. Mentally practice many times the sequence or climb that gives you the most problems. Remember that the physical practice of a sequence, when combined with mental practice, will yield much greater results than if you just physically worked it.

5. Create lots of strong positive images, while eliminating images of failure.

6. Create mental movies of yourself dealing with various situations or problems that might arise on a climb.

7. Work hard every day to change and reconstruct your negative and self-defeating images to positive and constructive ones.

8. Most importantly, establish a regular visualization practice schedule, just as you have a regular gym workout schedule.

---

see it through you own eyes. This creates a very detailed mental movie by dint of the tactile feel of grabbing holds and pulling through successive moves. The ultimate goal is total mind/body integration, best accomplished through creating these mental movies. (More on this in the table of visualization strategies) Visualization particularly is valuable when used to pre-program for an on-sight ascent. Be creative here. Visualize not only doing the moves, but placing the gear, chalking up, resting, and of course, topping out.

Conclusion

"All of these mental techniques give a climber a decided edge over someone who simply walks up to a route and climbs. As mentioned, said techniques are aquired skills, and initially require the same effort and disipline as working out in the gym. Once mastered, however, they require little time and effort to maintain. Practice them regularly and you're guranteed major improvements in your climbing skill; without them, you'll never realize your full potential. Remember that the best athletes are not those with something added, but rather those with very little of their potential taken away."

For best results, visualization should be practiced when you are relaxed and in a quiet place. Many short sessions each week are better than just one or two long sessions.

Climbers interested in further study should refer to the two texts used by Horst to fabricate his tables: *Mental Toughness Training For Sports,* by James E. Loehr, 1986, The Stephen Greene Press, Lexington, MA.; and *Health & Fitness Excellence,* by Robert Cooper, 1989, Houghton Mifflin Co., Boston, MA.

Our main man Eric Horst has plotted a clear and direct course for us to maximize our 'mental muscle.' Note that the course involves very specific techniques. We do not stare at a zircon pyramid, or at some plump guru's face and repeat a mouthful of hogwash. We not do consult *Zolatan's Astrology.* There is no wheatgrass or ethnic balm involved, no chanting to the moon. Just the basic, time-proven stuff here. Stick with Horst's techniques, and see tangible imporvements in your climbing. Guaranteed.

The only thing I might add is a little more slippery and far less defined. Should you have any spiritual convictions, orthodox or simply your own, quickly affirm them before starting up a route. All wise hearts, all creeds, agree about one thing – that life involves far more than climbing rocks. Be glad you're alive, healthy and with friends. Put the route in perspective. Granted, an extreme climb requires the tenacity of a polecat from hell; but it's still just a rock climb. If you hang your very identity on having to succeed, you only create undo pressures, and apprehensions of failing. If you're not afraid to fail, you probably won't. And if you can't nail the route that day, that hardly spells a washout. Who's stopping you from returning to try again another day? Never mind that Pepe de la Gaffo flashed the thing. To heck with Pepe and the burro he rode in on. Get relaxed, centered, visualize your success, acknowledge that climbing is a fabulous aspect of a multifarious life – but no more – then go after that route with a vengence!

Joshua Tree summit.
Kevin Powell photo

Evolution of a Champion

The world's greatest climbers started just like you and I did – by taking a beginner's class, holding a cousin's rope, getting pulled up a host of climbs by a friend. Sometime, probably early on, the champion makes the first important realization – that he (or she) loves climbing. He starts climbing more, masters basic ropework, and slowly hones technique. He might be a natural, but probably not. The most important ingredient is desire. If the desire endures, and he gets totally hooked, then it's full immersion – hitch-hiking to the boulders if there's no ride, climbing with anyone, anywhere, and boning up on all the literature down to analyzing guidebooks while on the toilet.

Soon, ill-defined goals are set – like breaking into doing 5.8. That accomplished, many routes are possible. The climber starts dreaming about scaling this one or that, and more tangible goals are drawn into focus. As the climber starts checking off the routes, and moving through the grades, his progress is pretty uniform, and increases relative to how much he climbs. The first major hurdle comes at 5.10. For years, this was the magic number, signifying entrance into a sort of mythical zone of difficulty. Though climbing 5.10 is commonplace nowadays, it doesn't seem so when a climber first gets there. These climbs are hard, and require a stout effort regardless of the climber's ability. The next phase is 5.11. Even today, when huge numbers are passe, the climber who can go to any area, climb any kind of rock at a 5.11 standard – from offsize cracks to slab routes – is a rare bird. The last hurdle is at solid 5.12, which is the threshold into world-class turf. Here, even the phenomenal natural athlete will really have to buckle down, because everyone regularly climbing 5.12 is a natural athlete. Moving past 5.12 requires raw toil and intense mileage on the rock; and even these cannot guarantee a champion. The key is the rarest ingredient of them all – the champion's mentality. Without it, the strongest, the bravest, the most talented natural climber ever born will never make a lasting mark. This mindset can be drawn out but never realized unless a climber has a little of it latently. One eventually will find out if he has that latent mindset, provided his desire is keen enough. It rarely is, however, because steadfast dedication is very hard to sustain.

The distractions and elemental needs of living in the 90s defeat most potential champions. Like most of us who set out to vanquish the climbing world, the aspiring champ will find it difficult enough just to keep his van running. It's a matter of money – or the lack of it – that keeps the bulk of us "weekend warriors" out of the running. The basic cost of living is so high that the bohemian life once enjoyed by 'crag rats' now is economically impossible. In the early 70s, a climber could go to Yosemite with a couple hundred dollars, climb the whole summer and drink beer every night. If you had $500, you could live like a Pharaoh, and maybe go on an expedition or two. But those days are gone forever, and anyone trying to live like that is pushed so far to the fringe of things that there is little distinguishing him from a bag person, kicking around the crags with a skimpy rack and a few cans of chick peas in his tattered pack. And that is no way to live. Moreover, it's virtually impossible to maintain a controlled and disciplined lifestyle – so essential for the world-class athlete – without a place to hang your hat, to cook, shower and relax. And even if you have the discipline and resources, even if you have the desire and God-given ability, so very few are willing to sacrifice virtually everything for climbing.

Almost to the man (and woman), those climbing at the very highest grade are, and have been, doing little else but climbing rocks for some years. They are fanatics who would never have gotten where they are if their climbing had not grown into a sort of all-consuming vice. Balzac said it costs as much to support a vice as it does to support a family. Those grappling toward the top will discover this; they must climb, climb, climb, at the exclusion of most everything else. There's little time for a job, a wife or husband, or even a fraction of what we know as the 'good life.' So you see, the odds are heavily stacked against anyone ever becomming a champion. A blown finger, a bad fall, a broken heart, feelings that life is passing him by – these things are lurking in the shadows, and virtually every champion must wage a pitched battle against any and all of them.

Yet despite all the hurdles and sacrifices, despite the million-to-one odds of it ever happening, a few champions always emerge. Through pure willpower, they kick down the barriers and give the rest of us things to marvel at. But the bona fide champion is more than just a fabulous technical climber. His best climbs are monuments to the human spirit, pivotal ascents that reorient and redefine the game. Because of this, he's a symbolic ambassador for everyone who owns a rope and a pair of boots. And he'll feel the heat of all the eyes upon him. The fool will say he could climb like that if he only had the time. The jealous, cowed by such passion, or suspicious of another's praise, will scoff and look for fault and shortcomings. He'll find them, of course, but he's missed the point – that it takes a miracle to become a champion. But how easy it is to criticize. A little wit, mixed with ill nature, confidence, and malice, will do it. But to everyone who has ever perused a guidebook or a ghastly cliff and dreamed a dream, it's the champion's face that smiles back at them, assuring us that he was the one who actualized the dream.

We don't worship him, because he's flesh and bone like all of us. For pure effort and remarkable accomplishment he deserves our praise; but he never demands it, for all the trials, failures and pain have shown him that even his success is modest and fleeting. Knowing that his victory is ours as well, the champion is gracious. He does not rub our faces in his prowess. Such a knave is not a champion, but simply a great climber. The genuine champion is far less vain than the climber who doesn't give a damn about who the champion is or what he's done.

The champion quickly will learn that it is much easier to become one than to remain one. It's never crowded at the top, but the queue is long and others are banging at the door. The game is for the young, and the champion can shine brightly only for so long. Realizing this, he attacks the crags with a mission, and makes his mark while he's hot. A little introspection will give him a sense of the proportion of things, so that when life finally catches up with him, he can climb on board. To doggedly try and hold out is not to live out a dream, but to foster a nightmare. The champion must realize when the time has come to move on. Not to is as tragic as if he had never climbed a single pitch. There are more things in life than climbing rocks, and he who thinks otherwise is bound to end up a loser, a bitter has-been hunkered down inside a wine bottle, for whom both climbing and life has passed by. After a time, he's unsuited for anything worthwhile. He simply didn't know when to get out and, like a fly in amber, he's stuck in no man's land. The champion, then, is the one who knows when he's done all he can, or all he should, and who gracefully passes the garland and exits the way he came in – inspired, staunch and true to the target. These things will hold him in good stead for the rest of his life. His victories have given him perspective. He leaves the sport in better shape than he found it, and we're all enriched by his contribution.

We'll still see him at the crags now and again. He'll climb as hard as he wants to, and we will all recognize him as the guy (or gal) who's having the most fun. No doubt, the authentic champion is the rarest thing in all the climbing world.

Big Wide Open Faces

. . . . The big wide open face, soaring out of sight, with nothing to slot your hands or feet into, no ready security but your wits. A thousand feet up and the ponderosa pines are so many shrubs below, the wide river a thin silver ribbon. You're above it all, and you feel like a god. The year, even the century, is meaningless. Then you clip a rusty, 20-year-old bolt, gape up at the 40-foot runout and again you're a sniveling mama's boy. Slowly, you cast off. Your belayer's eyes are two moons in a spooked face as you palm and smear and shake your way to that three-bolt belay, where you discover how the dead would feel to live again. And once more, you're in heaven.

There's an element of folly running through climbing rocks, brought home if you should ever break a bone or loose a friend. Ironic that such an unusual theater can summon the primordial being buried in us all, can throw us back to Java man, can make our feelings of fear and exhilaration basic, vital and real. Climbing the big wide open face cuts through the ages, pits us against our original selves – something only genuine range can do.

(opposite)
Middle Cathedral Rock,
Yosemite Valley.

George Meyers photo